Managing a Differentiated Classroom

A Practical Guide

Carol Ann Tomlinson & Marcia B. Imbeau

SCHOLASTIC

New York • Toronto • London • Auckland • Sydney
Mexico City • New Delhi • Hong Kong • Buenos Aires

Cover Designer: Jorge J. Namerow
Interior Designer: Q2AMedia

Picture Credits

4 Bonniej Graphic Design/Istockphoto; **8** Monkey Business Images/Istockphoto; **24** Comstock/Thinkstock; **36** Hannamariah/Shutterstock; **40** Jupiterimages/Brand X Pictures/Thinkstock; **60** Monkey Business Images/Shutterstock; **76** Comstock Images/Getty Images/Thinkstock
Q2A Media Art Bank: 25, 28, 30, 31, 34, 35, 38, 78, 79, 80, 82, 83, 84, 85, 86, 87, 88, 89, 91, 92, 94, 95.

ISBN: 978-0-545-30584-6

Copyright © 2011 by Carol Ann Tomlinson and Marci B. Imbeau
All rights reserved. Published by Scholastic Inc.
Printed in the U.S.A.

4 5 6 7 8 9 10   40   17 16 15 14 13 12

Contents

Introduction

> *"What would happen if we all always had to learn the same thing, at the same time, in the same way? Certain things would be way too hard for some of us and way too easy for others. I think a better thing is to be able to be myself and work in ways that work for me."*
>
> **Danyk, age 9, a student in a differentiated elementary classroom**

A colleague used to quip in presentations that he thought the only time there was such a thing as a homogeneous classroom was when he was in a room by himself. After an inevitable pause for audience laughter, he'd look quizzical and continue, "And come to think of it, I'm not even sure about that!"

He had a point, of course. A single individual may learn one subject easily and another with great difficulty, or approach unfamiliar content quite differently than content with which the person is comfortable.

As novice educators, some of us may have harbored an image of a classroom as a place in which our students would arrive as a matched set of learners, in sync with school, and ready to progress according to teacher plans. Most of us who entered the classroom with that image returned home without it by the end of our first day as a teacher. The idea of learner homogeneity has always been more a myth than an actuality. Nonetheless, we have clung to the myth in terms of classroom practice. It just seems "right" somehow that teachers should be able to create a single lesson, deliver it in a single way, adhere to a prescribed pace, and feel assured that our job is done.

Today's classrooms, however, reflect a degree of academic diversity that makes it nearly impossible for even the most habit-bound teacher to argue that student differences are insignificant in the learning process. Teachers may still teach as though all students in the classroom were essentially the same, but if learning is the measure of teacher success, one-size-fits-all instructional approaches are failing us. Too many students still can't read in fourth grade, and eighth grade, and twelfth grade. Too few students can reason mathematically. Too many students sit in uniformly taught classrooms and wait while the teacher re-teaches content to the whole group that a portion of the class mastered long ago. Too many students feel disconnected from learning or from the teacher or from their classroom peers—or all of the above. Too many students find school irrelevant to their interests.

It's not that teachers don't work hard. Most unquestionably do. It's that too many of us teach too often without a careful attention to the readiness range of the individuals before us, that we teach as though students' lives and interests are somehow outside the scope of our responsibility, that we too often teach in ways that are awkward for too many students. We need to learn to extend our instructional reach.

The good news is that the attitudes and skills necessary to develop a classroom that balances teacher responsibility for content and responsibility for young lives are not different from the skills of high quality teaching. They *are* the skills of high quality teaching! *And* they are skills well within the reach of most teachers. It's also good news that there has been vigorous and growing interest in developing what we've come to call "differentiated instruction" for well over a decade.

Still, too few classrooms are designed to make room for the very obvious differences students bring to school with them. Too few teachers consistently and proactively plan with students' varied learning needs in mind.

Research and experience in schools suggest clearly that many teachers who want to become more effective in differentiating instruction and who even understand with some precision what they could do to make their classrooms more responsive to student needs are reluctant to translate their desire and understanding into classroom practice because they feel uncertain about how to manage a classroom in which students are sometimes working with different tasks, materials, and timelines.

For anyone who has been a teacher, that apprehension is easy to understand. We recall the early-career fears that we would not be able to "handle" the students—that the classroom might suddenly erupt into chaos and that we would be totally inept in restoring order. For many of us, those fears emerged from nerve-taxing moments in the classroom that we don't care to remember or to repeat. The idea of a student-focused, flexibly managed, differentiated classroom seems an invitation to return to those novice days. In the absence of a clear sense of how to ensure the smooth operation of such a setting, it's easy to decline the invitation!

This is *not* a book on how to differentiate instruction. While the first chapter does provide a brief overview of differentiation, it is beyond the scope of this relatively short publication to address that whole topic. Rather, the goal of this book is to provide for teachers and other educators a tool for thinking systematically about what it means to guide and manage a differentiated classroom. To that end, Chapters 2, 3, and 4 describe both the goals of management in a differentiated classroom as well as nuts-and-bolts suggestions for directing a classroom that functions smoothly while providing flexibility for the students in it. The final chapter provides specific illustrations and resources to assist with translating the first four chapters into classroom practice.

The authors of the book are longtime educators who have taught in differentiated public school classrooms—one elementary and the other preschool, middle school, and high school—for a combined total of over three decades. Now at universities, we teach about and model differentiation for our adult students. Our experience brings us repeatedly to the dual conclusion that (1) effective attention to student variance is an imperative in contemporary classrooms if we concede that the only acceptable outcome of teaching is student learning, and (2) teachers of all levels of experience can—generally more easily than they think—become competent and confident in developing and leading a classroom that offers "learning room" for the young people they teach.

Another thought from a colleague is worth considering as we begin an exploration of what it means to "manage" a differentiated classroom. She cautioned, "Be careful not to confuse the edge of your rut with the horizon." Read and think along with us. Be willing to look further than yesterday's teaching practices. The horizon offers all sorts of possibilities.

Chapter 1
Differentiation: Reviewing the Basics

"This class taught me I have a choice about how I use my abilities. When I make the right choices, I can succeed and I feel better about myself. There's always another way to do things better if I'm willing to work with my teacher to find it. I never used to feel like I could be a success."

John, a student in a 6th grade differentiated classroom

The idea of differentiation must be at least as old as parenting. Few parents find they can raise multiple children in exactly the same way. Some children require more sleep and some less. Some eat everything put before them and some are finicky eaters. Some have even temperaments and some are more volatile. If one child develops a passion for music or for reading, it seems likely that the next one will find a niche in athletics or drama. Some children seem pre-programmed to do the right thing. Others seem to arrive with mischief in tow. Early on, parents learn that kids come into the world with their own agendas. Good parenting stems more often from helping one's children use those agendas wisely and well more than it arises from trying to formulate or re-formulate a child's agenda or nature.

It's much the same in teaching—except, of course, teachers don't have just two or three or four young agendas in the classroom. In today's classrooms, teachers are likely to work with students who

- learn rapidly and those who require much more time to learn;

- speak the language of the classroom and those whose first language is not the language of the teacher, the textbook, or of most peers;

- are compliant and students whose frustration with school or life or both results in negative behaviors;

- can sit and concentrate for extended periods of time and those who find it difficult to sit and listen for even a few minutes;

- have learning disabilities, autism spectrum disorders, cognitive handicaps, physical challenges, visual impairments, or some combination of those difficulties;

- come to school from privileged backgrounds with broad-ranging experiences and students from low-income backgrounds whose opportunities are few and whose challenges are many;

- represent many different cultures—often ones with which the teacher has little or no experience;

- learn as the teacher prefers to teach and those who find it nearly impossible to learn as the teacher prefers to teach;

- bring to the classroom widely differing strengths, interests and dreams; or

- represent several of these categories at once.

While most parents tend to quickly relinquish the idea that there is a single template for raising multiple children, teachers may be more inclined to cling to the hope that a single lesson plan, a single approach to teaching and learning, and a single timeline will somehow work for a classroom full of very distinctive young people. The result is too often a collection of disparate students who find learning awkward, distasteful, and even alienating rather than realizing its inherent satisfaction and power.

Differentiation is simply an approach to teaching and learning that recognizes the inevitability of academic diversity in contemporary classrooms and guides teachers in making decisions that attend to student differences rather than ignoring them. It suggests that teachers are more effective when they teach with student differences in mind and that students are the beneficiaries of such teachers.

What Differentiation Is NOT

There are many misconceptions about differentiation. It's helpful to consider some of them at the outset of an exploration of what it means to guide or manage a differentiated classroom. Figure 1.1 notes and addresses a few key misconceptions about differentiation.

As you continue to think about the concept of differentiation as it is presented in this book, think about other ideas that may be misconceptions. As is the case with students, teachers often have to address their own misconceptions before it's possible to accurately understand a concept.

Differentiation Is NOT...	Misconception Correction
New	The philosophy of differentiation is reflected in the writings of most of the world's major religions. It was standard practice in the one-room schoolhouse.
For a particular category of students (for example, special education, English learners, gifted education)	All students have specific interests, strengths, needs, points of entry, paces of learning, culture- and gender-influenced ways of learning. There is likely no student who won't benefit from focused teacher attention.
Something extra that teachers have to do in addition to their "normal" plans	Differentiation is not something a teacher does on top of "regular" classroom planning. Rather, it's a proactive approach to instruction that plans for student needs from the outset. It's not more planning. It's different planning.

Figure 1.1

Differentiation Is NOT...	Misconception Correction
Oppositional to content standards	Content standards are a curricular concern. Differentiation is an instructional approach. It suggests that whatever standards are determined to be essential, students will learn them better when the classroom makes room for their readiness, interest, and learning profile differences. Differentiation does not suggest different standards for different students, but rather provides different routes to achieving the required standards.
A way to "mollycoddle" students	Good differentiation always teaches a bit above a student's current reach and then provides support to enable the student to extend his/her reach. Good differentiation stretches students. It never waters down; rather it always "teaches up."
A particular set of instructional strategies	Differentiation is a way of thinking about the classroom, not a specified set of tools. There are many ways a teacher can attend to varied learner needs, and those can be responsive to student age, required content, and teacher personality.
Extreme teaching—something only an occasional teacher can be expected to do	The principles of differentiation are described as good practice or best practice by a broad range of professional organizations such as The National Board for Professional Teaching Standards, The National Association for the Education of Young Children, The National Middle School Association, and The National Association of Secondary School Principals.
Something teachers already do	Most teachers do attend to some student differences some of the time. Few teachers develop robustly and proactively differentiated classrooms.

What Differentiation IS

After studying differentiation for several months, Adam Hoppe, a pre-service teacher at the University of Virginia, proposed his own definition of the concept. He prefaced it by saying that he was sure there must be more to differentiation than he was seeing. His definition, he said, just seemed too "easy" to be correct. The definition he developed began, "Differentiation is a series of common-sense decisions made by teachers with a student-first orientation."

In fact, Adam's definition is absolutely correct. There's a common-sense logic to differentiation that seems so evident that it's difficult to contest. At its core, differentiation poses four questions to guide teacher thinking.

Core Questions About Differentiation

1. Is the environment in this classroom one in which every student will feel welcomed, safe, appreciated, challenged, and supported? Is this a place that invites learning?

2. Is it clear to both the teacher and students precisely what students should know, understand, and be able to do as the result of each segment of learning? Does the curriculum support both student engagement and student understanding?

3. Is the teacher consistently aware of each student's proximity to essential knowledge, understanding, and skill? Is he or she knowledgeable about students' interests and learning preferences? Do students increasingly know these things about themselves?

4. Does the teacher consistently use knowledge of student needs to plan instruction that addresses those needs?

While all this seem like the things that any good teacher would do, the truth is, of course, that consistently accomplishing the goals implied in the four questions is devilishly difficult. It's highly likely that even the most accomplished teacher falls short of the mark the questions imply on an almost daily basis. The goal of differentiation isn't perfection. Rather, it is to guide teachers who have the active intent to get better each day in connecting content and kids—in making sure each student learns as effectively and efficiently as possible.

HOW DIFFERENTIATION WORKS

DIFFERENTIATION is a **teacher's response** to a **student's needs**

Shaped by **mindset** and guided by **core principles** of differentiation

✓ Building Community
✓ Quality Curriculum
✓ Respectful Tasks
✓ Teaching Up
✓ Ongoing Assessment
✓ Flexible Grouping
✓ Flexible Classroom Management

Teachers can differentiate through
✓ Content ✓ Product
✓ Process ✓ Learning Environment

According to students'
✓ Readiness
✓ Interest
✓ Learning Profile

Through a variety of instructional strategies
✓ Complex Instruction
✓ Learning Centers
✓ Learning Contracts
✓ RAFT Assignments
✓ Sternberg Intelligence Preferences
✓ Tiered Activities
✓ Varied Homework
✓ WebQuests
✓ And other strategies…

Figure 1.2

Figure 1.2 shows the elements in a model of differentiated instruction and provides a line of logic for thinking about what differentiation is. The graphic begins with the assertion that differentiation occurs, at least to some degree, any time a teacher reaches out to address the particular needs of particular learners. It then shows how that might happen, introducing key principles, vocabulary and practices of differentiation. The rest of this chapter explores what is summarized in this graphic: core principles, classroom elements, and student needs and interests.

Core Principles of Differentiation

There are at least seven pivotal principles of effective differentiation. The list is not arbitrary, but rather reflects the philosophy behind differentiation, research that supports the model, and practices necessary for differentiation to work in a real classroom with real kids.

1 **A strong classroom community** supports learning for each of its members. Students learn better in a place where they feel respected and appreciated, where there is a sense of mutual trust among all members of the group, and where each student consistently encounters both high challenge and high support for accomplishing the challenge. Great classrooms function like the best athletic teams in that they come together around a common challenge, developing a sense of purpose, excitement, connectedness, and shared culture as they do so.

2 **Quality curriculum** belongs at the heart of every classroom. Such curriculum exhibits at least five characteristics. First, the teacher and students alike are absolutely clear on learning targets—precisely what students should know, understand, and be able to do as the result of any segment of learning. Second, quality curriculum focuses on what matters most in the content rather than accepting that the goal of learning is to absorb a maximum amount of data in minimum time. Third, quality curriculum helps students understand how content and the disciplines make sense, how they are organized, and how they relate to students' own lives and experiences. Fourth, quality curriculum asks students to use, apply, and transfer what they learn—in other words, to function at a high level of thought. Finally, quality curriculum is designed to engage students—to capture their imaginations, tap into their interests, help them realize a purpose in learning.

3 **Respectful tasks for all students** indicate respect for the capacity of all students. In other words, every student should have work that looks equally interesting and inviting. Every student's work should be understanding-focused. Every student should be expected to think (and be supported in thinking) at high levels. By giving these sorts of tasks to all students on a regular basis, teachers send clear signals that they believe all students can be achievers and productive thinkers.

4 **"Teaching up"** raises the ceiling for all students. The most promising differentiation occurs in classrooms where the teacher first plans for his/her most advanced students and then asks, "Now, how can I support other learners in achieving those complex goals?" Differentiation will inevitably yield the best results when teachers pay students the compliment of expecting more of them than they themselves believe they can achieve—simultaneously providing scaffolding, encouragement, and partnership necessary for students to accomplish what they once believed was beyond their reach.

All students, of course, will have some days when they simply need to practice a new skill or work with new information. No student, however, should be seen as only capable of drill and practice. The old approach of differentiation by Bloom's Taxonomy with some students working consistently at "low levels" of thought and some at "high levels" not only suggests a misunderstanding of the taxonomy, but a misunderstanding of how people learn.

5 **Ongoing assessment** informs responsive teaching. Once a teacher can specify what students should know, understand, and be able to do as the result of a unit, and can identify critical prerequisite knowledge, understanding, and skill that he/she assumes students bring to class with them, it's a short step to creating a pre-assessment designed to give the teacher a good sense of students with learning gaps that must be addressed, students who have advanced levels of mastery of the topic, and students who may have misconceptions that will interfere with learning. In addition, pre-assessment of student interests and

preferred ways of learning contribute to a teacher's evolving understanding of instructional approaches that will be most effective for the variety of learners in the classroom. Similarly, the presence of clear learning goals for each segment of learning makes it easy for teachers to use a variety of quick but effective formative assessment tools throughout a unit of study to keep a close watch for students who are ready to move ahead with learning, those who require additional practice, and those who need additional instruction individually or in small groups in order to progress appropriately.

Pre-assessments, of course, should never be graded. Formative assessments should rarely be graded. The purpose of both is to help the teacher and individual students chart and understand a successful learning journey. Assessments that are more summative in nature and with which students work at relevant points in a unit of study are appropriate for assigning grades. (Even summative assessments can be effectively differentiated in format and/or working conditions as long as the criteria for success remain constant and are tightly aligned with the unit's specified essential knowledge, understanding, and skill.) Students in classrooms with an effective formative assessment cycle should perform better on summative assessments because the formative information helps both the teacher and students understand students' learning trajectories and make adjustments necessary to push forward the learning of each student. For some classroom examples of pre-assessments and formative assessments, see Chapter 5.

6 **Flexible grouping** contributes to community and academic success. There are times in a differentiated classroom when students need to work with peers of a similar readiness level on tasks designed for their particular needs. There should also be frequent days when students work with tasks tailored to their interests and with peers who share those interests, regardless of readiness needs. There should be days when students work with tasks and peers that target similar learning preferences. On the other hand, there should be days when tasks are designed to bring together students of unlike readiness levels, dissimilar interests, or varied learning preferences. In these latter instances, tasks should be designed to ensure that each student can be a contributing

member of the group. In mixed readiness groups, for example, providing materials at varied readability levels may be important. In mixed interest and learning profile groups, tasks should be written so that particular strengths of each learner are necessary to complete the task effectively.

Differentiation should not become tracking inside the general classroom rather than externally. In other words, no bluebird, buzzard, and wombat groups! Students should regularly see themselves and one another in varied contexts. Flexible grouping also allows the teacher to "audition" students in a variety of settings and frequently spotlights previously hidden student strengths and interests.

7 **Flexible classroom management** allows the balance of structure and openness necessary for differentiation and for effective learning for the full range of students in a class. This principle, of course, reflects the purpose of this book. We'll explore the meaning and implementation of this principle throughout the remainder of the book. It's sufficient to note here that an effective differentiated classroom is well-managed using specific routines designed to ensure that there is "room" for each student in the class to learn in ways that match the student's needs while still attending to the needs of the class as a whole. Some educators reject differentiation based on the belief that differentiated classrooms are disorderly, if not chaotic. We trust you'll see as the book progresses that this is another misconception about differentiation, and that an effectively differentiated classroom is planned to ensure both order and flexibility that result in opportunity to learn.

Differentiating Classroom Elements

To the observant and reflective teacher, student needs emerge over the course of time through ongoing assessment, classroom observation, and conversations with and among students. The teacher's tools for addressing those needs are the elements in curriculum, instruction, and classroom environment. Those elements are typically called content, process, product, and learning environment.

Content

Content refers both to what students are expected to learn—what they should come to know, understand, and be able to do—and how students access the essential knowledge, understanding, and skill. Most of the time, in a differentiated classroom, teachers use the latter of those two options to differentiate content. Examples of differentiating how students access essential content include

- using materials in a student's first language;

- teaching or re-teaching in small groups;

- teaching in a variety of modes rather than in a single mode; and

- using resources matched to students' reading levels.

In at least three instances, however, teachers do differentiate the actual content. One of those occurs when a student's Individual Education Plan (IEP) indicates that he or she should work with a different set of goals than most of the class.

The second occurs when pre-assessments and formative assessments indicate that a student has critical gaps in content or when those measures indicate that a student has mastered content that the class as a whole is still studying. In the first of those instances, a teacher finds time in the day or week to systematically teach "backward," allowing a struggling student to accrue knowledge or skills that were prescribed for earlier years at the same time the teacher also moves the class ahead with new knowledge and skills.

A third instance in which it is appropriate for teachers to differentiate the actual content (vs. only access to the content) for students occurs when students already show mastery of content that the teacher has yet to teach, or again when a student masters new content much more rapidly than most classmates. A teacher who differentiates instruction should always plan to extend such students' proficiency with and use of essential content so that advanced learners can expect to grow throughout the year just as other students do.

In language arts or English, for example, a teacher may assign spelling or vocabulary words just beyond a student's current level of performance. Therefore, while all students work with spelling or vocabulary at the same time, some may be working with words at a primary level, some with words at an intermediate level, and some with words at a secondary level or even beyond. In a science class, a teacher may pre-teach critical vocabulary to a group of learners who struggle with academic vocabulary so that they are better prepared to deal with new content ahead. While a teacher should feel comfortable differentiating knowledge and skills when ongoing assessment indicates that some students would benefit from such adjustments, the big ideas, principles, or understandings that form the framework of meaning for the content should remain the same for virtually all students. Students may work with an understanding at different degrees of difficulty, challenge, or support, but understandings or big ideas make content meaningful and thus should be central to the work of virtually all learners.

Process

Process is sometimes used as a synonym for activities. Art Costa suggests using the term "sense-making activities." Early and often in the process stage of learning, students should stop being receptacles for information and begin to "own" the ideas by trying them out, applying them, transferring them, or connecting them to their lives, interests, or experiences. When students process information, skills, or understandings, they make those things their own. Processing should be the centerpiece of what takes place in the classroom because of its importance in learning. For that reason, much differentiation takes place during the process phase of an instructional cycle.

Products

Products might also be called summative assessments. They occur not at the end of a lesson or of a couple of days in the classroom, but rather after extended cycles of encountering new material (content) and working with the content (process). The term *product* appropriately suggests student output, or student demonstration of mastery of the essential knowledge, understanding, and skill specified for a period of weeks or even months. While there is a place for straightforward tests of content, products that have the most power to both extend and demonstrate student proficiency with essential content are "authentic." That is, they ask the students to use essential knowledge, understanding, and skill to address important issues or suggest solutions to meaningful problems.

Learning Environment

Learning environment refers to both the concrete and less tangible elements of the classroom. A teacher might make adjustments in the classroom environment itself in response to a student's affective or cognitive needs. For example, some students work more comfortably with peers than alone. Some students need supports to help them with organization. Some students need more structure in their day while other students would benefit from greater autonomy in decision-making. Some students might benefit from working in an area of the classroom where there are no visual stimuli that could be distracting. Learning environment adjustments can include time, space, materials, and room arrangement as well.

Differentiating in Response to Student Needs

Both research and classroom experience affirm that students come to school with differences in at least three key areas that can significantly impact learning—readiness, interest, and learning profile. Teachers in a differentiated classroom use ongoing assessment to construct an understanding of how all three areas affect their students. Then they adapt the classroom elements (content, process, product, and learning environment) to address the three areas of student variance (readiness, interest, and learning profile). It is possible to modify each classroom element in response to each area of student variance. For example, a teacher can modify process or activities to respond to student readiness needs, to student interests, and/or to student learning profiles.

Readiness is *not* a synonym for ability. It refers to a student's current proximity to specific learning goals, targets, or outcomes. It is possible for a student to be a very quick learner and still struggle with a specific aspect of math or to be behind for a time in Spanish because the student was out of school for a week with the flu. In trying to understand student readiness, a teacher simply asks the question, "Given what students should know, understand, and be able to do at the end of today (or the end of this week), where is this student now and what will he or she need in order to succeed with the goals?" There is ample evidence that students cannot learn—they cannot grow academically—when work is consistently too hard or too easy for their entry points into the work. Quite literally, only when tasks are in an appropriate challenge range for a particular student can that student progress and achieve.

Interest has to do with a student's proclivity for a particular topic or endeavor. Once again, both research and classroom experience indicate that interest ignites motivation to learn. There are a number of ways teachers can tap into student interest. One, of course, is to make lessons generally interesting. Another is to show students how required content links to their unique interests. For example, a student who may not care for poetry might change his mind if a teacher allows the student to find poetry at work in a kind of music the student loves. A student who has difficulty with math may be encouraged to use important mathematical concepts if they show her how she might get a better deal on a cell phone bill. A student who is talented in art may be more inclined to invest heavily in a social studies project if he can use some techniques and tools of art that he aspires to master. It's also possible to have students select from a list of required topics in a unit the one in which he or she would like to specialize. By using strategies like expert groups or Jigsaw, students explore the topic of their choice in greater depth. This can often open the door to deeper interest in the topic as a whole.

Learning profile is an umbrella term related to several factors that shape individuals' preferences for how to approach learning. The term reflects our current knowledge about learning styles (for example, preferences for learning through hearing or reading, in a darker or lighter room, beginning with parts and moving to wholes or vice versa), intelligence preferences (based on the work of Howard Gardner and Robert Sternberg, who suggest the brain is hard-wired to learn better in some ways than others), culture (which shapes ways in which individuals see and respond to the world around them),

> " Students come to school with differences in at least three key areas that can significantly impact learning—readiness, interest, and learning profile. "

and gender (which again tends to shape individuals as learners). In attending to student learning profile, it is wise to steer clear of hard-and-fast approaches. For example, while there are certain learning preferences that are typical of males, it is not the case that all males learn in the same way or that females don't learn in those ways. It is the case that members of some cultural groups are reflective, for example, and value thinking at some length before they speak or act. That is not true of all members of those groups and is a characteristic of many learners who do not belong to those cultural groups. A student may appear to be a visual learner much of the time, but may, in fact, learn new things best by hearing rather than reading about them.

In short, differentiating instruction in response to student learning profile is not about labeling and assigning students to certain learning "categories" or "styles." Rather, it's about creating a range of learning opportunities in the classroom from which students may select. The teacher then helps students reflect on their choices with an eye to consistently understanding themselves better as learners and making increasingly better choices about learning for themselves.

Instructional Strategies for Differentiation

There are an infinite number of instructional strategies a teacher can use to reach out to a variety of student needs in the classroom. (Within the scope of this book we cannot provide comprehensive descriptions of such strategies, but we have provided a list of recommended additional resources on page 96.) Some of the strategies are especially well suited to addressing readiness needs. Among those are tiering, small group instruction, learning contracts, learning centers, and resources at varied readability levels. Other strategies work especially well in addressing student interests. Among those are Jigsaw, independent studies, WebQuests and web inquiries, and orbitals. Likewise, there are a number of approaches that lend themselves well to addressing student learning preferences, including designing tasks that offer analytical, practical and creative options (based on Robert Sternberg's Triarchic Theory of Intelligence), providing multiple options for expressing learning in project or product assignments (as long as the learning goals remain constant across the options), and giving students the choice of working alone or with peers.

It's possible, of course, for a teacher to develop tasks for students that attend to readiness, interest, and learning profile simultaneously. One example of an instructional strategy that attends to all three student needs is RAFT assignments. RAFT assignments are writing projects designed to help students understand their Role as a writer, the Audience for whom they are writing, the Format in which they will write, and the Topic they will write about. An example of a RAFT assignment differentiated to address student variance in readiness, interest, and learning profile is included in Chapter 5.

In fact, a number of the strategies noted above can be useful in addressing more than one type of student need. For example, learning contracts can be used to attend to readiness, interest, and learning profile needs. Centers can be constructed to address readiness and/or interest. Often the most effective strategies are not ones that have been created and named by others, but rather strategies developed by teachers to match both the requirements of content and the needs of students who, at a given moment and in a particular setting, are expected to learn that content.

You may have noticed that there is one item in Figure 1.2 that we omitted from this brief overview of differentiation. Near the top of the diagram is the suggestion that differentiation begins with a teacher's mindset. We'll examine that idea in Chapter 2 as we begin to explore the specifics of leading and managing a differentiated classroom.

Chapter 2
Preparing for Differentiation

"If everybody had to learn the same thing in the same way at the same time, it would be too easy or too hard, because everybody is different, not the same. Thank goodness it's not like that in our classroom!"

David, age 10, a student in a differentiated elementary classroom

There's actually nothing particularly complex in guiding a differentiated classroom—as long as a teacher is willing to plan thoughtfully. In some ways, making a differentiated classroom work is a bit like playing chess or checkers. You need to have a clear goal in mind, develop strategies for achieving the goal, be observant and reflective as you go to ensure that the game plan is working as it should and adjust when it's not.

This chapter will examine three aspects of planning to guide a differentiated classroom.

1. Preparing the teacher
2. Preparing students
3. Preparing the classroom

Brief surveys at the beginning of the three sections should help you think about your current status in each area as you read and think about how to move ahead with differentiation in your classroom.

Planning to Prepare Yourself for Differentiation

Before you read further in this section, take a look at Figure 2.1 and mark the column you believe best reflects your current status or position for each statement. That should help orient you to the discussion that follows.

Survey 1	I'm really solid in this area	I'm moving in the right direction	I haven't thought about it much	This could be a problem
My students would say I believe they are all capable of academic success.				
I understand the principles of differentiation.				
It's my job to make sure every student learns what matters most in our content.				
My belief in the worth and dignity of each student shapes my thinking and actions in the classroom.				
I can explain my beliefs about why differentiation is important.				
I see myself as a leader of my students.				
I see myself as a team builder in the classroom.				
I'm an effective manager of details in the classroom.				

Figure 2.1

> **Most students can learn most things if they are willing to work hard and if they are supported in doing so.**

The most important element in a differentiated classroom is not the nature of the room, the quality of materials and supplies, the class size, or the schedule. It's a teacher who continues to hone his or her craft until the classroom works for each of the learners in it. Such teachers are likely to have two core convictions that propel their work.

The first is a belief in the value of each student they teach. They understand the potential of the teacher to shape young lives and accept the teacher's obligation to ensure that all aspects of their work contribute to positive development for each student.

The second is an abiding belief in the potential of each student they teach. They have what psychologist Carol Dweck calls a "fluid" or "growth" mindset. That is, they believe that most students can learn most things if they are willing to work hard and if they are supported in doing so.

These two bedrock principles lead teachers to a series of conclusions that guide their actions in the classroom.

Guiding Principles for the Differentiated Classroom

- **It is impossible to respect an individual while simultaneously seeing the person's differences as problematic.**

  Therefore, these teachers seek to create classrooms in which student differences are viewed as both natural and desirable.

- **Learners of any age are inspired by adults who believe in them.**

  Therefore, these teachers see themselves as mentors of the young people they teach. They invite students to do important things and provide a context in which students see themselves rise to challenges they once believed were beyond their reach.

- **Learning happens most effectively in a setting where every student feels safe, known, and valued.**

  Therefore, these teachers teach young people to respect one another, support one another's growth, celebrate one another's accomplishments, and share responsibility with the teacher for the success of classroom operations.

- **A teacher must know students as individuals in order to understand how to teach them most effectively.**

  Therefore, these teachers study their students as enthusiastically as they study the content they teach.

- **A teacher's hard work on behalf of each student and the teacher's insistence on hard work from each student will result in highly positive outcomes for each student.**

  Therefore, they work hard to make instruction a good fit for each student and insist that their students work just as hard on their own behalf

In reality, of course, few teachers have perfect days—ones in which everything goes absolutely as planned and all students experience maximum growth. Differentiation and teachers who practice it simply subscribe to the premise that there is always another way to think about teaching and learning that just might be more effective in helping a student succeed, and that it's the teacher's role to continue to grow in order to benefit the young people they teach. If that's the case, the teacher should have or be developing

- a belief system that suggests attending to learner differences is important for student success;

- the intent to create a classroom environment that invites each student to learn and supports each student in doing so;

- clarity about curricular goals that ensure student engagement with and understanding of essential content;

- a variety of ways to get to understand students better;

- an understanding of differentiation as an instructional model that will support fidelity of implementation; and

- a desire to design classroom routines and structures that balance predictability and flexibility.

It's important to note again that you need not have mastery or certainty in each of these areas before beginning to differentiate. Rather, it's necessary that you see the importance of each of these areas in reaching the full range of students and that you are a willing learner in each of them.

Preparing Your Students for Differentiation

It's time for your second survey. To help yourself think about what you may need to do to help your students prepare for a differentiated classroom, look at the survey on the next page. Consider each statement and mark the appropriate box.

Survey 2	I'm really solid in this area	I'm moving in the right direction	I haven't thought about it much	This could be a problem
I talk with my students regularly about why we are doing what we are doing in the classroom.				
I explain to my students my beliefs about teaching and learning.				
My students would say they help me create the kind of classroom we want to have.				
I regularly seek input from my students on how the classroom is working for them and act on what I hear.				
My students see themselves as my partners in making the classroom work effectively and efficiently.				
My students are comfortable in helping one another appropriately when someone needs assistance.				
I have some good ideas about how to explain differentiation to my students.				

Figure 2.2

Most of us have had the experience of playing a game like Scrabble or Monopoly with someone whose understanding of the directions for the game is different from our own. The game becomes punctuated with comments like, "That's not how you do it," or, "That's not right." It doesn't take long for the game to go bad and feelings to go sour.

With the possible exception of preschoolers, most students also enter classrooms with a clear set of internalized rules about how to "do school." Those rules are typically artifacts of one-size-fits-all classrooms and include beliefs like the following:

1. Everybody starts and stops work at exactly the same time.

2. Everybody uses the same book, does the same homework, and has the same projects and tests.

3. When kids have questions, they should ask the teacher for help.

4. Fair means everybody is treated just alike.

If a teacher uses an occasional, modest differentiation strategy in a classroom, that's not likely to create a major problem for students in terms of their perception of the rules of the "school game." However, if a teacher wants to make significant progress in terms of creating a differentiated classroom, the rules of the game will necessarily be different than the rules the student may have brought to the classroom.

For example, in a differentiated classroom, students will not always start and stop tasks at the same moment. They will not always use the same book or do the same homework, or have the same project or test. They will need to learn to help one another appropriately when they need assistance rather than only relying on the teacher.

In order to avoid the problem of different conceptions of rules for the same game, it's important for a teacher to prepare students for what may be a new set of rules. That begins with helping them understand not only what the new rules will be, but also why they matter. To accomplish this, it's helpful for teachers to plan a three-part discussion in which students consider the following ideas.

> If a teacher wants to make significant progress in terms of creating a differentiated classroom, the rules of the game will necessarily be different than the rules the student may have brought to the classroom.

Three-Part Discussion Plan
Introducing Differentiation to Students

Part 1: Understand that the students in their class are both alike and different as learners—and that a good class will take into account both the similarities and differences.

Part 2: Think about how a classroom that honored all the students in it would look and function.

Part 3: Begin to consider the roles and responsibilities of teachers and students in such a class.

Discussion Part 1
Who We Are

As the teacher begins to learn about students in the very earliest days of the school year, it's helpful to develop a way to have students reflect individually and as a group on themselves as learners. Simple activities like the following two can be woven into everyday classroom instruction to accomplish this.

Appreciating and Learning About Our Differences

Elementary Example

A teacher of elementary students who were about to study geometric shapes decided to use the concept of squares and cubes in order to help her students understand how unique they were. She began by giving each student a set of six one dimensional squares that were attached in a template that could be folded into a three-dimensional cube.

Each square had a number from one to six printed on it. Students were given a set of directions. They were told, for instance, to color square 1 light blue if they thought they were really good with spelling, lavender if they were pretty good with spelling, and dark blue if spelling was hard for them. Likewise, they were asked to put stars on square 2 if they were really good at kickball, check marks if they were pretty good at kickball, and X marks if they found kickball to be hard for them. (See Chapter 5, page 83, for instructions and another example.)

When students completed their squares and assembled them into cubes, the teacher asked them to find all the other cubes of other students that were just like their own so they could collaborate to make mobiles that contained identical cubes. It didn't take the students long to figure out that the mobile project wasn't going to work. There were no two cubes in the class with the same colors and markings on six facets.

Appreciating and Learning About Our Differences

Middle School Example

A teacher asked her students to stand on a masking tape line on the floor to reflect their individual agreement with statements she made. Statement **1**, for instance, was, "I am really quick at solving word problems." Statement **2** was, "I'm very confident of my skills in converting decimals into fractions." Statement **3** was, "I learn best when I work in a small group with other classmates." Students who strongly agreed with the statement stood toward the left of the line, those who strongly disagreed stood toward the right of the line, and others distributed themselves along the line as they thought appropriate.

The teacher took a digital photo of each continuum prior to posing the next question and asking students to move based on their response to the question. (See Chapter 5, page 81, for the full list of questions.) The teacher posted the continuum photos by class period and asked students in each class to study the photos and jot down any conclusions they could draw about sixth graders and math based on the photos. Their responses included things such as, "Some sixth graders will probably do really well with fractions and some will probably have trouble with them at first," "Some sixth graders really like working in small groups and some don't," "Sixth graders have very different strengths and weaknesses in math," and so on.

In both activities, the teacher's goal was to have students conclude that there were many differences among them as learners, and also some similarities. See Chapter 5 for more detailed explanations of these and other activities to help you get to know your students.

Discussion Part 2
A Classroom That Works for Everyone

The teacher's next step is to engage the students in a conversation about how a teacher should teach when students have different strengths, different weak points, different interests, and different ways of learning. With very young students, you may simply say, "Because every one of us is different, we will sometimes need to have different ways to learn things. Let's talk about how that might work."

With slightly older students, you might ask, "What are some things I need to do when I'm planning lessons to make sure everyone has a chance to learn in a way that works for them?" With upper elementary and middle school students, you might ask, "How should I teach when your strengths and interests, and needs, and ways of learning are so varied? Who should I be thinking about when I plan?"

Students will nearly always be clear that if a teacher is just thinking about and planning for one kind of learner, the class won't work well for others. They will often suggest, for example, that a teacher should help students develop their individual strengths and work on their particular weaknesses, or that a teacher might need to teach in more than one way.

As the conversation evolves, you can guide students in talking about what the classroom might look like if it were designed to help each student learn as much as possible and in the best way possible. Some typical student responses might include:

- "We might be reading different books."

- "We might meet with the teacher in small groups to work on something that's important for those of us in the group."

- "We might show what we are learning in different ways."

It's fine to contribute to the discussion. For example, you might ask, "Can you think of times when it might be helpful for students to be able to move on to new work when they've finished learning what we're working on instead of waiting to move on when everyone else does?"

Discussion Part 3
About How to Make the Classroom Work

Ultimately, it's wise to begin having students consider how everyone would have to be part of making the classroom work smoothly when different things are going on at the same time. Among common student responses are

- "We would have to be sure to listen to our directions instead of somebody else's or we'll get confused and never finish anything."

- "We couldn't interrupt the teacher if she was working with other students, so we would have to help one another."

- "We'd have to be sure that we were working quietly enough for other people to think about their work."

Middle schoolers might suggest, "We'd need to make sure the room is straight when the bell rings to go to our next class."

It is useful for you to point out some ways in which you will need students as partners in making the classroom work well for everyone. Depending on particular student, content, and teacher needs, student help might include such basic tasks as: passing out and collecting materials, checking in homework, making sure materials and supplies go back where they belong when students finish using them, moving furniture quietly and quickly, carefully following directions in centers, and helping you think of ways to make the classroom more effective for everyone.

All three parts of this discussion should begin at the outset of the year and continue throughout the year. Discussions early in the year will likely take longer than ones later in the year that will generally serve as reminders of class purpose and goals, checks on how well various aspects of the class are working, or opportunities to extend or refine earlier understandings. In all instances, some messages will remain constant:

- Everyone in our class is important.

- It's important for every person in our class to be a strong learner.

- Our goal is for everyone to learn as much as possible as quickly as possible.

- We all sometimes need to learn in different ways.

- We can create a class that allows students to work in ways that work best for them it as long as we work as a team to make that happen.

No matter when the conversations occur—but particularly early in the year when students are extra-vigilant in establishing how the teacher relates to them—it's critical to

- demonstrate respect for every student;

- ensure that every student has a voice in the conversations;

- take each student seriously and be sure that students take each other seriously;

- be a good listener;

- remind students of their shared goal of a class that works for everyone;

- be a celebrant when things go well; and

- be clear about the need to do better when they do not.

Preparing the Room for Differentiation

As you begin to consider the role your classroom space might play in differentiation, take a look at Figure 2.3. Where is your thinking currently in regard to the items on the checklist? Given what you understand to be the goals of differentiation, can you anticipate why your answers to the individual questions might be important as you move ahead?

Survey 3	I'm really solid in this area	I'm moving in the right direction	I haven't thought about it much	This could be a problem
The room has designated spaces for materials and supplies so students can access them and return them easily.				
I use space and furniture flexibly in the classroom.				
There is space for me to meet with individuals and small groups of students.				
I use wall and bulletin board space to display student work.				
There are places in the room dedicated to providing guidance for quality student work.				
There are places that help students know assignments, schedules, and seating arrangements.				
I use classroom space to help build community or a sense of team.				

Figure 2.3

A classroom is really just a box—four walls, a floor, a ceiling, some furniture, and some supplies—but there is considerable power in what we decide to do with the box. As is the case with a room in a house, we can design a classroom in many different ways. Some encourage flexibility in addressing learner variance and developing student autonomy, others less so.

Among "design decisions" that can be quite useful in supporting differentiation are the following.

> "A classroom is really just a box—four walls, a floor, a ceiling, some furniture, and some supplies—but there is considerable power in what we decide to do with the box."

Furniture

- It will likely work better to have a single-student desks and some tables or clusters of individual desks rather than all of one or the other. This allows space for students who need to work alone some of the time. It also allows space for collaboration, which is an important feature in a differentiated classroom.

- Develop floor plans or seating plans for several different furniture arrangements—for example: an arrangement for a whole class discussion in which students sit in a square or circle so that everyone can be seen and heard, an arrangement for working in pairs or triads, and an arrangement that provides some seating for small groups and some for individuals.

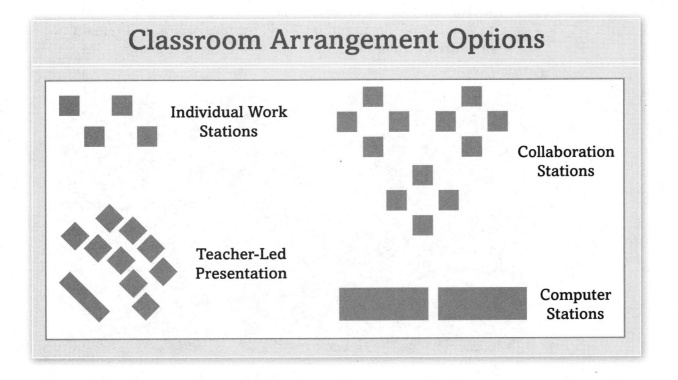

Classroom Arrangement Options

Individual Work Stations

Collaboration Stations

Teacher-Led Presentation

Computer Stations

- For young learners, it's especially important that there is a space in the room where students can sit on the floor as a whole class to talk together, listen to stories, plan the day, and so on.

- In elementary classrooms, strongly consider "permanent" spaces for learning and/or interest centers. In middle school, consider a furniture arrangement for "stations." You might assign students to stations on a rotating basis for varying lengths of time during portions of a unit in which different learners would benefit from different practice tasks, application tasks, skills practice, and/or small-group instruction.

- Be sure to have a space in the room where small groups can meet with the teacher while other students work on assigned tasks at their desks. The space should allow students who are working with the teacher to sit with their backs to the rest of the class and allow the teacher to easily see everyone in the room.

- Create a space in the classroom where desks can be turned away from visual stimuli (including movement of other students) to help students who need to work without visual distraction. Providing earphones or ear plugs for students who are significantly distracted by sound can also be quite helpful.

Supplies and Materials

- Use easy-to-reach "organizers" such as stack trays, bins, crates, shelves, or boxes that students can access as needed. The goal is to enable students to submit work, retrieve papers, and remain organized with minimal direction from you once routines are in place.

- Think about color-coding or using icons to designate subjects or class periods. For example, in middle school, first period has blue folders or manila folders with student names written in blue marker and stored in a blue crate. In elementary school, students might turn in science work to the yellow tray, math work to the green tray, and so on. Using colors and icons can be helpful to young students, English learners, and a variety of students with reading difficulties.

- In all grades, provide subject- and age-appropriate materials that allow students to explore and express what they are learning in a variety of ways. These might include reading and reference materials, art supplies, videos, and writing materials, for example. While the materials may vary during the year, it's good to designate space where materials are predictably available and can be retrieved and returned in an orderly way.

- It's important to have one or more areas of the room for reading materials (as well as audio and Internet content) that address a range of reading levels and interests. Again, the materials may change to supplement various units of study, but students should know that there will always be things they can read or listen to in order to support their learning.

- Plan spaces for technologies students will use. These might include digital recorders, computers, Braille readers, cameras, or tablet computers. This area should balance a need for security and for student access.

- It's often extremely useful to have a permanent "anchor activity" station in the room. Anchor activities are tasks to which a student moves when an initial task is completed. They will be discussed further in Chapters 4 and 5.

- Plan spaces for materials and supplies that only you should be able to access. These should be out of the way of student traffic, less noticeable to students, and clearly designated "for the teacher only."

Wall and Other Display Space

Use available wall space and other display areas for two purposes: building community and supporting learning.

- Consider using some wall or display space to spotlight students throughout the year. Let students work with you to bring in or create artifacts that share their interests, strengths, accomplishments, and goals. Use the space as a way for the you and your students to get to know and appreciate one another better.

- Use some wall space to display student work that demonstrates noteworthy effort, growth, and/or quality. This helps students understand that their work leads to growth, and to new levels of success.

- Use a designated section of wall and/or table space to post rubrics or checklists for quality as well as student work that exemplifies the specified criteria at various levels of challenge or sophistication. You might then ask some students to

1 Do I understand the model of differentiation?

- *Do I know what it is and is not?*

2 Do I know why it matters to create a differentiated classroom?

- *Why will it be worth the effort?*

- *Why is it necessary to the success of my students as learners and my success as a teacher?*

3 Do I see myself as a leader of my students?

- *Am I prepared to inspire, encourage, and support them more than to "manage" them?*

4 Am I prepared to enlist the partnership of my students in creating a class that works for everyone?

- *Do I know what that partnership means and am I prepared to help my students understand what it means?*

5 Have I made the best possible use of space to support community, flexible teaching and learning, organization, and escalating student autonomy?

- *Will the classroom set-up and structures work for or against the goal of maximizing the success of each learner?*

examine the work mounted on orange paper, and some to examine the work mounted on yellow paper, for example, to see how quality student work looks in a unit on which they are currently working.

- Consider having a "first aid station" or "life saving station" in the room. In this area, you (or the students themselves) would post reminders that could enable students to work successfully on a current task if they have forgotten certain skills from earlier lessons. For example, a help poster might remind students how to convert a Word file to a PDF file on the computer or how to write a lab report. The idea is to enable students to do related tasks successfully and with minimal assistance.

In preparing for a differentiated classroom, you should be confident in answering the questions on the preceding checklist affirmatively.

Once again, there is a difference between being ready to begin a process and being perfect. Thoughtful teachers will not only continually find better ways go about their work because they learn from experience, but they will draw energy from their capacity to grow as professionals. The goal at this point is not absolute certainty about how each detail will play out, but a sense of preparedness to approach the starting gate.

In addition to preparing the teacher and students to understand the principles of differentiation and preparing the room to facilitate enacting those principles, it's important to develop routines that enable students to work with the right balance of structure and flexibility. Chapter 3 will explore some routines found in many effectively differentiated classrooms as well as the thinking behind those routines.

Chapter 3
Establishing the Routines of Differentiation

> *"In my class, our teacher says we have to work hard so we can be smart and we all have to help each other be smart too. We try to help our teacher make sure the classroom runs right so it helps us all be smart."*
>
> Maria, a student in a
> 3rd grade differentiated classroom

Many categories of people are charged with "leading and managing" the work of others. When they are successful, their success stems from a number of common attributes. Certainly part of successful management stems from the kinds of ideas we've explored in earlier chapters—such as having and communicating a vision of a quality outcome, operating from a clear sense of direction, respecting and believing in those whom they direct, working hard, and establishing an ethic of hard work among the group.

Beyond those crucial if somewhat abstract attributes, good leaders and mangers are attentive to detail. They plan assiduously. They don't leave much to chance.

Think about a school football coach who starts the season with a group of disparate adolescents and forges them into a team on which everyone knows the game, understands the game plan, knows his role in executing the plan, and learns when to focus on his own role and when to support others in doing their jobs. Or consider the orchestra conductor who brings together players of significantly different instruments, helping each member become more attuned to his or her instrument while simultaneously directing them in playing shared, sectional, and solo parts.

The successful coach and conductor have knowledge of and enthusiasm for their craft. They lead. They encourage, exhort, and demand.

They also plan doggedly with the intent to effectively focus on the myriad of seemingly insignificant details that ultimately yield a potent opponent on the field, a powerful listening experience in the concert hall, or a riveting drama. The devil is in the details! Success is in the persistent execution of those details.

This chapter will center on six important elements that, if carefully planned and thoughtfully executed, enable teachers to focus on both the needs of individual learners and the needs of the class as a whole. More to the point, when these elements work for teacher and students, both are more likely to succeed! These are the elements, which form the framework for this chapter:

1. Setting an effective classroom tone

2. Getting to know students

3. Using anchor activities

4. Establishing ground rules and routines

5. Using small groups

6. Staying organized

Some teachers may already feel confident and competent in some of these areas. Others may require additional thought, planning, and practice to lead as effectively as they would like in these areas. Most teachers have room to grow in most of the areas. As we do grow, we become better stewards of the responsibility of teaching students who need us in different ways.

Setting an Effective Classroom Tone

Students typically enter classrooms that are new to them with their antennae primed. Well before they ask what the content will be, they are seeking an answer to a question that is typically more important to them: "What's it going to be like in here for me?"

Classrooms that harness the imaginations and energies of young people reflect a dynamic tone that is first established through a series of messages, evolving customs or rules, and teacher modeling. The messages begin with the teacher and should convey the sense that this classroom is a happening place where people matter, ideas are important, hard work is necessary, and success is expected.

Figure 3.1 displays some of the critical messages students should receive early and often about their classroom, what the messages mean, why the messages matter, and how teachers might convey them. Ensuring clarity about these messages over time helps students develop an understanding of how differentiation works and why it matters. It also paves the path toward a classroom that maximizes the potential of each student.

The Message	What It Means	Why It Matters	Some Ways Teachers Can Convey the Message
You matter to me, individually and as a group.	• You're on the radar here. • You have a voice. I hear you and want to hear you. • There will be no anonymous people in this class.	• Students need to feel valued by important adults in their lives. • They need a sense of affiliation with a group. • They need to know that what they bring to the classroom is valuable.	• Making small segments of time available for teacher/student conversation. • Being at the door as students come and go. • Referring to student comments, suggestions during instruction. • Going to student events. • Calling on students randomly rather than responding to raised/waving hands.

Figure 3.1

The Message	What It Means	Why It Matters	Some Ways Teachers Can Convey the Message
What we learn here is very important.	• We're going to think about ideas the way experts do. • We're going to learn things in ways that help you see their value in the world. • There are so many important ideas that we'll have to use our time well. • You're going to see yourself in what we learn.	• Young people rally behind things that seem important and purposeful. • People learn best when ideas are relevant to their experiences.	• Showing students how people beyond the classroom use the ideas and skills they learn. • Connecting content with students' varied interests and experiences. • Showing students how the ideas and skills make people's lives better. • Making sure students use what they learn to act on problems and issues. • Sharing stories of experts in the content areas from different cultures and both genders.
Every person in the class has a key role to play in the success of all of us.	• The class belongs to all of us, not just to the teacher. • The teacher is more effective when the students are her partners in making the classroom work. • You can count on me, and I'm counting on you. • Every student has strengths that benefit us all.	• Responsibility builds self-confidence. • Pulling together as a team fulfills a need for both affiliation (belonging) and agency (making a difference). • The teacher cannot do everything without help.	• Giving students responsibility to facilitate classroom operation. • Talking with students regularly about why you do what you do in the classroom. • Seeking student input on how to make the classroom work better. • Acknowledging and celebrating things that are working well.

The Message	What It Means	Why It Matters	Some Ways Teachers Can Convey the Message
Everyone will work hard in here because that's what makes us all successful.	• The teacher works hard to support your success. • You will work hard to support your own success. • Stay busy. • No shortcuts. • Quality work is an expectation.	• An emphasis on hard work rather than ability increases the likelihood of student success. • Students develop greater respect for themselves when they work toward high expectations. • Developing pride in craftsmanship benefits all students.	• Being sure students see you hold high standards for yourself and for them. • Talking frequently about student effort and seldom about ability. • Using models of quality student work. • Writing directions that emphasize quality. • Making sure rubrics emphasize quality vs. quantity or baseline expectations.
Growth is a non-negotiable.	• Incremental growth is the route to meaningful achievement. • Everyone has their own next steps to take in learning every day. • You will be expected to take your next steps every day. • In life and in class, there is always the opportunity for growth.	• Persistent effort leads to growth, and growth enables students to master and exceed expectations. • Competing against oneself is the fairest and most important contest in life. • We fare best when we accept responsibility for being the best we can be.	• Emphasizing personal growth rather than interpersonal competition. • Teaching students to set personal goals and establish plans to achieve them. • Acknowledging and celebrating growth in each student. • Discussing students' mastery of essential goals, habits of mind and work, and progress toward mastery when talking to parents.

A second part of setting a classroom tone that is conducive to differentiation—and to effective teaching in general—is establishing rules or guidelines or agreements for classroom behavior. The rules and the process of arriving at them becomes a sort of shorthand for what will follow. Consider the following:

- The rules are for teacher and students. Students should not be asked to act in ways that do not consistently reflect the teacher's attitude and behavior.

- Involve the students in developing the rules that will govern them.

- Work to make the list of rules as short as possible. For example, four very terse guidelines that cover just about everything are:

  1. Respect yourself
  2. Respect one another
  3. Respect this place
  4. Work hard

  If a teacher and his or her students consistently aspired to those standards, the classroom would model the world most of us would like to live in.

- Be sure students have an opportunity to talk about why particular rules or guidelines are important for their individual success and the success of the class as a whole. Rules should exist to support success, not as arbitrary demands.

- Review the rules with students every once in a while. Join them in reflecting on how well they are working for individuals and the class and in deciding how to make sure the rules are working as they should to support the success of each student.

A third element in establishing a classroom tone that supports academic success is a teacher who consistently models what he or she asks of students. The teacher is continually aware that he or she must be for the students what he or she wants the students to be for one another. Here are some examples.

- If you expect students to be respectful of one another, you must be respectful of every student all the time—in class and out. Your humor must be positive. It must be evident that you enjoy, value, and listen to each student. The students cannot conclude that you see some students as winners and others as losers. If you hold students to standards of hard work, persistence, and craftsmanship, the students must see those attributes in you every day.

- If you tell students that effort and solid habits of mind are more important than getting everything right all the time, you must exemplify that mode of operation—and must pay more attention to those characteristics in students than you do to points on a test or rank in class.

- If you make a case that the talents, strengths, and experiences of each student are valuable, you must make instructional plans that draw on a full range of abilities and experiences in ways that make them visible and valuable to the class.

In many organizations, both commercial and professional, there is much talk about "branding." They ask the questions such as these:

- What do we really stand for?
- How can we convey that in a memorable and clear way?
- How can we be sure we deliver on our promise—that we are who we say we are?

Establishing a classroom tone that speaks of, promotes, and supports the academic success of each member of the class rests in large part on those same questions and on the ability of the teacher to answer them appropriately on a personal, professional, and practitioner level.

Getting to Know the Students

A genuinely daunting aspect of teaching is getting to know students as individuals. It seems overwhelming to try to understand a group of 25 or 30 elementary students. It seems impossible to know 125 or 150 secondary students. Nonetheless, there may be no more important challenge for a teacher. It is difficult to connect with students who feel anonymous. It's nearly impossible for students to trust a teacher in whose classroom they feel faceless and unknown.

A teacher's investment in knowing and understanding students as individuals yields big dividends. Students feel acknowledged, significant. They draw the conclusion that this teacher is a person who has their best interest at heart—someone who will make the risk of learning less daunting. As students see the teacher reach out with interest and respect to their peers as well, they begin to build trust and respect among themselves as well. The result is the beginning of a sense of community in the classroom—the weaving of a fabric that supports learning.

If working to know students as individuals fosters trust, working to know them as learners enables better teaching. Noted educator Hilda Taba once said that teaching in the dark is questionable business. Nonetheless, we often do that. We assume a student can read the material we provide, or that she knows vocabulary or math skills that were taught in past years, or that our upcoming lessons will provide him with new information. Too often, however, some students can't read the materials, don't have prerequisite knowledge and skills, or have already learned what we are about to teach.

We forge ahead with our plans as though those issues didn't exist. The result is not only an academic misfit, but the erosion of trust with our students. As one middle school student noted, "That teacher doesn't have any idea what my life is like. She doesn't even know that I don't have a clue what she's talking about in class. Why should I care when she doesn't?"

There are three words that describe the process of teachers who get to know their students as people and as learners: purposeful, planned, and persistent. They intend to know the people they teach for the purpose of teaching them more effectively. They see the process as personally and professionally rewarding. Because the individuals are many and time is short, these teachers plan ways to learn about their students. They also understand that the process of getting to know students will necessarily be evolutionary, and so they begin the process as the year begins and stick with it until students leave at year's end.

> **There are three words that describe the process of teachers who get to know their students as people and as learners: purposeful, planned, and persistent.**

How to Be Students of Your Students

- **Learn Their Names**

  Learn students' names as quickly as possible as the year begins. You could play name games, ask students to decorate name tents to place on their desks for a week, or take their pictures and create a visual seating chart that you can study even when you're not in the classroom.

- **Let Them Know You Want to Know Them**

  On the first day of school make it evident to your students that you are actively learning about them. This could be as simple as going around the classroom and asking students to share "one interesting thing about you or what you like to do." Comment on their responses and take notes on what they say. Use what you learn to shape your instruction, and let students know you are doing that. For example, you might say, "I know a lot of you like graphic novels, so why don't we make our own?"

- **Meet With Them**

  With young students, use morning or afternoon meetings to encourage students to share with you and with one another. With older students, take a minute or two as class begins or ends to talk with students about things that matter to you, and invite them to do the same.

- **Have Them Write to You**

  Consider using journals in which students can write to you informally about interests, needs or concerns.

- **Reach Out Beyond the Classroom**

  Go to students' extracurricular activities. Invite parents to share their insights about their sons and daughters.

- **Gather Information About Them**

  Develop surveys so students can share interests, strengths, talents, preferred ways of learning, and hopes for the year. Ask students to update the information later in the year. (See Chapter 5.)

- **Greet Them Individually**

  Stand at the door every day as students enter and leave the room and make contact with them individually.

- **Observe Their Work**

  Walk around the classroom as students work independently or in small groups. Make notes of problems students may be having and of students whose rapid and accurate performance may indicate that they are being under-challenged. Again, use what you see to shape instruction, and let students know you are doing so. (See Chapter 5, page 93, for an example of a mini-lesson in response to a classroom observation.)

- **Have Quick Chats**

  Have brief, informal conversations with individual students about extracurricular topics to help you understand them beyond the classroom.

- **Track Their Progress**

  Develop ways of keeping track of student progress, such as skills sequence charts, sticky note folders, and bio-checks. (See Chapter 5.) This process allows you to keep track of student status on essential content goals even when they engage in varied activities. It can also be very helpful in preparing for parent conferences and conversations with students about their work.

Getting to know students isn't about becoming a social worker or a counselor, and it isn't an accessory to the role of the teacher. Your facility in getting to know students in a three-dimensional way is the first step in building a community of learners; it allows more precise and targeted instruction; and it develops the your long-term understanding of how to connect content and kids.

Using Anchor Activities

It's rare in any classroom that all students complete an activity or an assessment at precisely the same moment. In a differentiated classroom, the idea of "ragged time," or students completing work at different points, is a given. Anchor activities are tasks to which students move automatically when they are finished with assigned work. These activities enable teachers to use time flexibly by ensuring that students have productive work to do when they complete a task.

What Is An Anchor Activity?

Anchor activities should have the following characteristics:

1. The work is significant in enhancing the students' knowledge, understanding, and/or skills related to the year's content.

2. The work is interesting and appealing to students of a particular grade and age.

3. Students can complete the work without help from the teacher.

One of the most familiar types of anchor activities is a journal. Students are told that whenever they have "down time," they should add an entry—something they've learned, a song lyric they heard, a question they want answered. You can also put intriguing journal prompts on the board each day such as a question, a sentence starter, or a story starter.

- *What would happen if there were no television?*
- *If I had a superpower, it would be _____.*
- *One night, a tiny spaceship appeared over the roof of the house next door.*

For more anchor activity ideas, see pages 87–89 in Chapter 5.

While introducing anchor activities to students, it's important for them to understand the nature and purpose of the activities as well as procedures and expectations for working with anchor tasks. It's helpful to convey the following ideas at appropriate times.

- Anchor activities are designed to be interesting to students. They provide an opportunity for students to learn things they might not otherwise have the chance to know about the subjects they are studying.

- Some anchor activities may stay constant through the year (for example, books, magazines, or websites to read about a topic the students are studying). Others will change after a period of days or weeks.

- You will be happy to hear suggestions from students of anchor activities that seem useful and interesting.

- There are so many important things to learn that there's never a reason to say, "I'm finished with my work and I don't have anything else to do." A student should automatically move to an anchor activity when they finish assigned work.

- Anchor activities won't be graded, but you will be observing how effectively students work with them. This information will be part of your conversation with students and parents about habits of mind and work. Be sure to let students know if they should keep a record of their anchor work or respond to it in any way. (See Chapter 5, page 90, for an example of an anchor log.)

- If a student feels "stuck" in trying to complete an anchor activity, he or she should read accompanying directions carefully, see if there are samples or models of student work at the anchor activity station, see if a peer can help, or select a different anchor activity until you are available to help.

- Anchor materials should not go home (not leave the classroom) with students unless the teacher gives permission.

- Students will need to return anchor materials to the anchor activity station when you announces that it's time for a transition to new work or a new class.

Different teachers will begin anchor activity routines in different ways, depending on their own comfort with a flexible classroom and the age and nature of the students with whom they work. Some teachers may be more comfortable offering only one anchor activity when they are introduced, and may want the activity to be one that students do with little or no movement or conversation. Other teachers may prefer to have two or more choices from the outset so that students learn to manage choices as the year begins. Similarly, these teachers may be comfortable with students moving around the room quietly to access varied materials and working with a partner on anchor tasks. What matters is that students understand the purpose of anchor activities and how to succeed with anchor routines—whatever they are in a particular teacher's classroom.

Establishing Ground Rules and Routines

One key to the success of a flexible classroom is a set of routines that students understand well and execute with consistency and confidence. To ensure that these routines are effective and efficient, establish a set of ground rules that apply to most or all of them. Soon the routines will simply become "the way we do things in here."

There is no single set of ground rules for all settings. Rather, teachers should reflect on how they feel their particular classroom should operate. Among areas for consideration are the following, several of which will be explored further in Chapter 4.

GUIDING QUESTIONS FOR ESTABLISHING ROUTINES
How will you start and stop class, or segments of lessons?
• You may decide that the school bell signals the start of class, or you could devise a special signal to indicate that students should be in place and ready to begin work. This signal can be a word or phrase from you, a specific time on the clock, or a humorous sound from a noisemaker.
• When the bell rings or the signal is given, what should that mean? Should students already be seated with work materials in place, or does the signal indicate that they have a specified length of time to move to their seats and get ready?

- Think about how you will conclude class or a segment of class. You may want to give a signal a few minutes before the end so that students have time to take care of certain tasks or activities. For example, you can establish that this time is used to wrap up or turn in work, or to return materials and supplies to their proper places in the room. Or, you may choose to use the last few minutes for a quick formative assessment and/or a brief conversation with students.

Will there be times you are "off limits" to students?

- Decide when students should feel free to talk to you, and when they should know that you are "off limits." For example, is it okay for students to interrupt you when you're working with small groups or individuals, or should they wait?
- When class is beginning, or when students are moving from one activity to another, do you want to be able to move freely around the classroom to make sure students settle in well, or is this a good time for students to come to you with questions and comments?

What should students do when they need help and you are busy?

It is a given that students will have questions or need help when you are occupied with another individual or group. What routines can you establish that will help them get that help on their own? You could

- emphasize listening to or reading directions carefully so that students are more likely to understand what they need to do at a given point from the outset of the task;
- have examples of student work available in the classroom to serve as models students can consult;
- have recorded directions so students can go to a digital recorder and re-play instructions, or assign an "Expert of the Day" who can assist students with particular aspects of their work when you are unavailable to help them.

Recorded !! instructions

If a student has made every effort to understand a task and is still unable to move forward, is there a way that student should indicate a need for help? (See Chapter 5, page 94, for examples of color-coded help signals). Should the student move automatically to an anchor activity, or is there a different alternative for productive use of time?

How should students get help from their peers?

- Asking classmates for support is a helpful strategy for almost every student. But you probably don't want unrestricted conversation all the time. Consider these questions, and make sure students know the ground rules you decide on.
- Are there times when you really want students to help one another and times when it's not appropriate (for example, during informal assessments)?
- When is it okay for one student to decline helping another student, and how can he or she do so in a respectful way?

- Do you prefer that students seek help only from students seated near them, or is it okay for them to go across the room for help?
- How long can a student continue to sit and work with another student, and when should a help-seeking or help-giving student return to his or her initial seat?
- What level of voice is appropriate when asking for help or working together? Note that these rules may change depending on the activity or context.
- When should students decide on their own whom to ask for help, and when should they only go to certain individuals like the Expert of the Day?

What are the rules for using materials?

- Are there materials, supplies, or areas of the room that students are free to access at any time?
- Are there resources students should not use unless instructed to do so by you?
- How should students care for materials, supplies, and the room itself?

What do you expect of students in terms of movement around the classroom?

- When are students free to get out of their seats to get materials, turn in work, or to consult with a peer or with you? When should they remain in their seats?
- When students are up and moving around the room, do you expect them to go directly to their destination, or is it acceptable to stop along the way to chat with others or look at things?
- If a group of students need materials or have a question, can multiple group members get up to handle the need, or would you prefer to that one student from the group obtain what's needed?

For collaborative tasks, how will students know where to sit or whom to work with?

Assignment charts, pocket charts, and classroom maps are all useful tools. Other options are color coded-lists of student names posted on chart paper or projected on the wall via projector, or colored slips of paper that are given to students with the direction that they find teammates with the same color. Consider these questions as well:

- How often will groups change?
- When should students check the charts?
- Will you signal when it's time to move to the designated areas and tasks?
- What should students carry to their new location and what should they leave at their initial seats?

Addressing all of these categories at once, of course, would be overwhelming you and your students alike. Students would be confused, and the class would seem like a rule factory. Rather the goal is for you to deal with the details the way an effective coach, conductor, or director would—thinking about the desired outcome (from your perspective, what a smoothly functioning, student-focused classroom should look like), and introducing and attending to the details as necessary to achieve that outcome.

Using Small Groups

Using small instructional groups is not an imperative for differentiation per se, but it probably is for effective instruction in general. Most students are motivated by working with peers. They need the sounding boards their peers can offer. Some students really only learn well when they can talk out their ideas with a classmate.

Working with peers helps student take stock of their work and work habits relative to that of others. Certainly, in today's increasingly diverse society, it's important for students to be aware of the perspectives of others and to learn to work with and appreciate the contributions of all kinds of people. Further, the capacity to work and solve problems collaboratively is a skill most young people will need in the world that will belong to them. In addition, it's much easier to think about planning tasks for a few groups than to plan for 30 or so individuals.

Despite the potential power of small-group instruction in the classroom, effective group functioning is clearly not automatic. Students generally don't come to school knowing how to be an effective group member or how to deal with issues that can arise when students work together. The same might be said of teachers, of course.

Groups are most likely to work effectively when the teacher develops tasks and gives directions for those tasks with group needs in mind, and when the teacher actively teaches students the skills of collaboration as those skills are called for in student work.

Considerations for Group Success

- Task goals, expectations, and working parameters are clear to students.

- Students understand the teacher's expectations in terms of quality work.

- Students understand fundamental practices of group behavior, such as listening, taking turns, explaining one's perspective, setting goals, making plans, summarizing, monitoring progress, blending several ideas into a solution, and encouraging one another.

- Students know how to get help if they need it along the way—both individually and as a group, and both in terms of group process and the task at hand.

- When there are group roles (for example: time keeper, materials monitor, note taker, etc.) students understand their role and how it relates to other roles as well as to accomplishing the group's task.

- The task is interesting to the students who are asked to complete it.

- The task is designed in such a way that it calls on the strengths of each member of the group in order to complete the task well. Tasks should not be crafted in such a way that some students can complete them with little effort and others have little hope of completing them or contributing to them.

- All students in a group should have a worthwhile academic contribution to make to a quality outcome.

- The task requires genuine collaboration for successful completion.

- Timelines for the task are brisk, but not rigid.

- Individuals are accountable for their own work, but also for explaining all facets of the task and the work of others in completing the task.

- There is an escape hatch or a way out of a group for a student who cannot succeed with the group. This may be pre-arranged with the teacher and students who have difficulty with peer interactions or it may be presented by the teacher as needed. (Often, the solution is simply having the student work on the task independently in a spot in the room that allows the student mental and physical space to regroup.) The alternative should always preserve the dignity of the student who is leaving the group and should be handled with the expectation that it is a temporary solution. It should not be punitive.

- Students know what to do when the group's work is finished, including next steps (perhaps an anchor activity to be completed individually), and where/how to turn in their work.

Often as teachers we err in expecting that we will need to teach students content, but not processes. That rarely turns out to be a helpful assumption. In designing and using group work in a differentiated classroom, plan to teach both. Be as clear in coaching students in group membership as you are in science, math, art, or other content areas students will use in the group. Observe students as they work in groups. Take notes on what you see. Point out to students what you see them doing effectively in groups and help them understand why their behaviors were beneficial to the group's success. When their group work is less effective than it needs to be, be clear about that as well. Ask students to help you analyze the problems and pose solutions. Always take time to have students reflect on both their work and their process when they work in groups. Like most other aspects of classroom success, there is a direct connection between a thoughtful and thorough teacher and positive outcomes.

Staying Organized

A significant part of organization stems from the kind of pre-planning suggested in this book. When teaching is grounded in a carefully considered philosophy and model, when a teacher has well-defined learning goals in mind and has clear mental images of how the classroom should be working to enable each student to succeed, organization is far more likely than when teaching is a fly-by-the-seat-of-the-pants proposition. In the former instance, teaching is largely proactively planned. In the latter, teaching is a largely reacting to the moment. There are, however, additional steps you may want to take in a differentiated classroom to support organization.

Consider Home Base Seats

In many elementary classrooms, students have assigned or home base seats. They begin and end the day in these seats, but move to other seats during the day as necessary for particular assignments. In middle school, it is probably less often the case that students have assigned or home base seats. Middle school teachers sometimes feel that allowing students to choose where to sit is respectful of or helpful in supporting students' increasing independence. In a differentiated classroom at any grade level, home base seats can be a great organizational tool. When students begin and end class in assigned seats, you see the following benefits:

- It's easier to learn student names early in the year and to systematically study their students as the year begins.

- You can develop seating arrangements that are conducive to focus, concentration and support for each student.

- You can take attendance while students work rather than taking time each day to "call the roll."

- It's easier for you or designated students to distribute materials or supplies as class is beginning.

- It's easier to monitor clean-up at the end of a class segment.

- There is a structure and predictability about how class will work that benefits many students.

Explain to students that they will not spend a great deal of time in their home base seats because they will often need to work at other places in the room. Help them understand why home base seats should make the class work better. Encourage them to talk with you if they feel their home base seat is not working well for them.

Assign Roles for Classroom Responsibilities

There are many roles students can play in effective classroom functioning. For example, they can

- check in student work;

- move furniture to allow flexible use of classroom space;

- distribute and collect student work folders, materials, and supplies;

- straighten areas of the room at the end of a class segment or at the end of the day;

- assist with classroom displays or setting up for labs or other student tasks; and

- make sure equipment is working effectively.

Role charts that specify tasks and match students to them are an efficient way to assign roles. It generally makes sense for a student to keep the same role for at least a week or longer.

Consider Using Pre-assigned Groups

Some instructional groups will need to change almost daily in an effectively differentiated classroom. However, there may be some student groupings that should remain constant for a month or even a marking period. In those instances, it's a time-saver to assign the groups at the outset of the time span and let students know who the group members will be. (Always note that you may make a few adjustments in the groups as student needs evolve.) Here are three examples of groups that may be effectively pre-assigned.

1. **Synthesis or Summary Groups** These are groups of three or four students who meet together briefly at key points in a learning sequence to review key ideas or check comfort with important skills. In many instances, it's helpful to use heterogeneous readiness groups for this purpose.

2. **Brainstorming Groups** These groups of three or four might meet periodically as students work on complex products or writing assignments. They serve the purpose of generating initial ideas for student work, helping peers troubleshoot when they get bogged down with carrying out their ideas, and helping one another look at ways to enhance the quality of their work. It's important that each group includes at least one student who is effective in generating original ideas and at least one who understands how to work for quality. It might be useful at some points to use groups that are homogeneous by student interest.

3. **Literature Circles** These groups, which often have five or more members, stay together through the reading of a shared novel. Roles of group members may revolve or remain constant as the group discusses what they are reading. Membership in these groups is typically based on reading level and/or shared interest in a novel. Such groups can easily be adapted for use in discussing readings from any subject.

The point of organizational structures in a classroom is not to create rigidity; rather, organization should lead to flexibility. When both teacher and students understand with precision how things work in the classroom, routines become automatic and working with content moves to the foreground where it should be.

Guidelines for Establishing Routines in a Differentiated Classroom

- **Focus on the vision and rationale for differentiation.** Most of us as humans, students included, are willing to follow procedures and engage in routines that make sense to us—that serve a common good. We are less inclined to follow a set of rules because "somebody in charge said so." Present procedures and routines as a method of supporting student success. Procedures and routines that don't serve that purpose should likely be jettisoned.

- **Give students a big voice in making the classroom work.** The classroom needs to be a place that belongs to everyone in it. For that reason, everyone in it should have a consistent voice in making it work as well as it possibly can.

- **Don't overload students with procedures and rules.** Do begin the process of establishing routines on the first day of school, but teach them at a pace that enables students to master a few of them before moving on to others. Your goal should be able to honestly say to students at the end of a day or a week, "You did this really well. I'm proud of you." Asking too much too fast makes that goal difficult to achieve.

- **Practice routines.** Most of us learn better what we do than what we hear. Have students walk through—or at the very least explain to one another—how a particular routine should work.

- **Teach students the skills they need to succeed with routines and procedures**. It would be stellar if students all came to school knowing how to listen, plan, ask helpful questions, keep track of their work, move furniture, be respectful, and so on. Young people have to learn those things as they go. Any time a teacher notes that some students lack those critical competencies, the only sensible response is to teach them.

- **Hold high standards of quality for execution of routines and procedures.** If the classroom culture is to be one of excellence (and that should always be the case for all students), teachers need to persist in helping students achieve quality performance in classroom routines and procedures—as well as in math, music, history, reading, and so on.

- **Be specific and reflective.** Make sure students know exactly what is expected, why you're asking it of them, and how all of you will know whether something is working well. Review expectations and standards of quality periodically (more often early in the year, less often later). Take time to discuss with students their perceptions about how particular processes are working and to get their ideas for improvement. Be specific in both praise and correction regarding routines and procedures.

A teacher who takes the time to understand the nature and intent of differentiation and to invite students to contribute to a classroom that works for everyone, establishes a physical environment that supports attention to individuals as well as increasing student ownership of learning. In addition, a teacher who develops thoughtful routines to ensure smooth classroom functioning, generally feels comfortable and confident with beginning to manage a responsive classroom. However, there are still some questions commonly asked by teachers new to differentiation. Chapter 4 will provide some of the answers.

Chapter 4
Frequently Asked Questions

"If it weren't for differentiation, we would have no challenge at all. Lots of people have lots of different learning abilities. Without differentiation, we would be frustrated..."

Shaun, age 9, a student in a differentiated elementary classroom

A teacher who learns to manage a flexible or differentiated classroom is, in many ways, an educator who learns to balance. For example, such classrooms reflect a balance between: structure and freedom, teacher voice and student voice, requirements and student needs, whole class and small group instruction, the needs of the group and the needs of the individual, planning and flexibility, common goals and individual goals, and so on.

Because of a fundamental fear of "losing control" in the classroom, it's easy to favor structure, teacher voice, requirements, whole-class instruction, the needs of the group, planning, and common goals. In shifting toward a classroom that is geared to success for a full range of learners rather than success for "generic" learners—in other words, in learning to strike a balance— it's necessary to relinquish more familiar classroom processes characterized by teacher frontal control and student absorption in favor of greater student participation and meaning-making. It is not, however, necessary to give up a classroom that functions in a smooth, purposeful, and productive manner.

This chapter will focus on questions teachers often ask as they seek to move their management style to one that is more responsive to the needs of a full range of learners. As teachers develop clarity around these issues, they are increasingly able to collaborate with students to develop a classroom that makes room for all kinds of learners. The questions that follow are common among teachers new to the concept of differentiation. The answers provided to those questions are ones that would likely be given by teachers for whom differentiation has become a comfortable and productive way to teach.

Won't There Be More Discipline Problems in a Differentiated Classroom?

A common fear among teachers who are new to the idea of differentiation is that discipline problems will increase in a differentiated classroom because students have more freedom. There is no guarantee that differentiation (or any other factor) will eliminate all student misbehavior or convert all young people into consistently judicious decision-makers. Nonetheless, effective differentiation virtually always reduces discipline problems rather than increasing them for at least three reasons.

First, many students misbehave out of frustration arising from instruction that is a poor fit for their learning needs. Work may be regularly too easy or too hard for a student. The pace of instruction may be too fast or too slow. Content and tasks may seem detached from their experiences. The teacher's mode of instruction may be a mismatch for their preferred ways of learning.

When a teacher works to address students' varied readiness levels, interests, and learning preferences, the likelihood of such mismatches decreases, student success increases, and the need to act out declines accordingly.

Second, effectively differentiated classrooms regularly communicate to students that they have the capacity to impact their own success. Teachers emphasize effort as the pathway to success rather than ability. Clarity about learning goals and criteria for success make it more likely that students know what it will take to do quality work. Students, like teachers, examine formative assessment information to help them chart a path to success. Further, students help one another achieve quality outcomes. And, again, instruction is designed to address students' varied learning needs. All of these factors give students increased efficacy as learners. When people have an internal locus of control, or a sense that they are in charge of their own destiny, the need for misbehavior again declines.

Third, in effectively differentiated classrooms, students learn how to use classroom routines in ways that support their own learning and that of their peers. More to the point, they have a voice in establishing and refining the routines and understand how they support student success. Those elements support positive behavior as well.

One teacher explained concisely why differentiation generally alleviates rather than contributes to student misbehavior. He said, "When the system works for a student, the student no longer feels a need to work the system."

Certainly there will still be occasional instances of misbehavior in almost any classroom. An effectively differentiated classroom makes it easier for you to handle those instances for the following reasons:

> **When the system works for a student, the student no longer feels a need to work the system.**

1. Most students are focused on and challenged by their work.

2. The classroom has a positive tone of high expectations and high support that enlists positive attitudes in most students.

3. When the majority of students work effectively in small groups or independently, you have time to work with behavior issues.

In instances of misbehavior, it's important for you to understand what causes a student to misbehave. That understanding leads to solutions that are effective for the student, the class as a whole, and the teacher. Even in acute situations when it is necessary to remove a student from the classroom, it's valuable for you to act in a way that preserves the student's dignity and to follow up by seeking to understand the problem in order to work with the student in addressing its underlying causes.

In some settings, a large number of students come to school from stressful homes, having felt alienated by school for an extended time, lacking fundamental skills for school success, and/or lacking basic skills of group membership. While teaching classes that are largely or exclusively composed of such students can be extraordinarily challenging, these students, like all others, need a classroom where they are greeted with high regard and positive expectations, that is responsive to their learning needs, and that teaches them both the academic and personal skills needed for success in and beyond the classroom.

Helping these students move toward greater autonomy as learners requires a teacher who is simultaneously accepting and demanding, sometimes called "warm demanders." These teachers establish very clear expectations for student respect and behavior, and insist on student compliance with those expectations. The compliance, however, is not for purposes of teacher control, but rather to ensure an environment in which students can thrive both academically and personally. Students, therefore, interpret the teacher's insistence as a sign that the teacher both cares for and believes in them. "Warm demanders" do not inhibit, but rather build toward, a setting in which students not only learn but also learn how to learn with increasing autonomy.

How Will I Know My Students Are Learning If I'm Not Watching Them All the Time?

Young people (and people in general) learn because the tasks in which they engage are meaningful to them, the work they do is interesting, and/or what they do gives them a sense of power and possibility. Watch them tackle a new athletic skill, a new piece of technology, or a new game.

It's not necessary for an adult to "supervise" their every move for them to learn. In fact sometimes they learn more readily when adults step back and let them "own" the situation.

Likewise, in a differentiated classroom, students will learn because the work they do is a good match for their learning needs, tasks are interesting and relevant to their experiences, they are clear about expectations and indicators of quality, and/or they are encouraged as learners by the sense of trust and autonomy shown them by the teachers.

Teachers certainly should move around the classroom as students work as often as feasible, talking with students about what they are doing and "spot-checking" their work, but is not necessary to stand over students or to observe them from the front of the room as a condition for learning.

How Will I Know Who Has Mastered a Skill If Students Do Different Tasks?

When a teacher is clear about the essential knowledge, understanding, and skills required for success in a given lesson, it's simple to create a matrix of those requirements and use it to monitor student mastery. (Chapter 5, page 91, provides an example).

Move among students as they work, examining what they are doing to determine who is and is not working comfortably with a particular skill. For example, a second-grade teacher may look at student work (even if the work is not the same for everyone in the class) to see who is and is not writing in complete sentences.

A middle-school science teacher may, for example, need to know whether a student can demonstrate cause-and-effect relationships. The student might demonstrate mastery of that skill in a lab report, a project, an oral report, a class discussion, or a formative assessment, to name a few possibilities. The teacher simply records the date(s) on which she observed the student using the skill appropriately, and perhaps the context in which she made the observation.

In a differentiated classroom, four students demonstrate mastery on a pre-assessment, six others on an early formative assessment, ten in a lab report, and some others not until a final product or test. The issue is not *when* a student shows mastery or in what format, but rather that each student ultimately masters essential content and that you are aware of each student's status relative to essential goals.

How Do I Give Directions When Student Tasks Vary?

If students have differentiated assignments for which the directions are the same, it's simple to give instructions for the assignments to the group as a whole. However, when tasks vary enough so that directions are different for various groups or individuals, it's generally wiser not to go over multiple sets of directions in front of the whole class. Doing so is time consuming, confusing to students, and calls too much attention to task variety. Below are some approaches that can be used instead.

1. **Use Task Cards.** A task card is a sheet of paper or large index card that gives directions to a group or individual for their assigned work. Task cards can include general directions, criteria for success, time parameters, student roles—anything you'd normally tell students to support their success.

Map Task Card 1

Use your map to answer the following five questions about U.S. rivers. There are books on your table that can help. Be sure your answers include the key unit vocabulary about maps and geography so you are writing like an expert would about the topic.

1. Which river runs north to south and divides the country in half? How did you determine the best answer to this question?

2. What rivers form state borders? Which states do they border? What determines which states have particular rights to the shared rivers?

Map Task Card 2

Use your map to answer the following five questions about U.S. rivers. There are books and articles on your table with important passages marked to help you. Be sure your answers include the key unit vocabulary about maps and geography so you are writing like an expert would about the topic. Use the graphic organizer on your table to help you be sure you have good information on all the parts of the questions.

1. Which river runs north to south and divides the country in half? How did you determine the best answer to this question?

2. What rivers form state borders? Which states do they border? Explain and give examples of several ways the rivers help all of the states they border.

2 **Use Recorders.** Sometimes it's easier to record directions for students rather than write them out. Recorded directions also allow students who don't read comfortably to access directions, and they have the added benefit of allowing students to re-play the directions as an assignment progresses to be sure they're on track if a task is complex or multifaceted.

3 **Give Directions in Advance to One Student in Each Group.** There are always students who listen well, remember what they hear, understand directions, and enjoy helping peers. You can go over directions for a specific task with this kind of student the day prior to or a short while before students are assigned the task, making sure the student can repeat or paraphrase the directions accurately. The student then relays the directions to his/her group when students assemble in designated spots in the room to complete assigned work.

4 **Use a Mixture of Strategies for Giving Directions.** Some groups might work well with task cards while others might benefit from recorded directions. Most groups might effectively use student directions-givers while there may be a group where students struggle or where a task is quite novel or complex that would work more effectively if you gave directions to the group in person.

How Do I Manage Time in a Differentiated Classroom?

In a class that is not responsive to student variance, teachers ask everyone to hand in an assignment at the same time and expect them to move readily from one unit of study to the next at the designated time. It is not accurate to assume, however, that in those settings students are all in the same place at the same time in terms of their knowledge, understanding, and skill. It's simply that we've grown accustomed to moving ahead "by the clock" without a great deal of regard to that reality. It's time to collect the papers, so we do that. It's time to move to the next unit, so we do. In a differentiated classroom, the difference is that the teacher tries to honor two realities: the need for maintaining a reasonable pace and the needs of students that may not be well served by a rigid pace.

There are two aspects of time management in a differentiated classroom that raise questions for teachers new to differentiation. First, what if some students finish their work early during a class segment or period? Second, what if some students still need more time on a particular topic and the teacher feels he or she must move on to the next topic? There is a third question that should arise, but does so less often than the first two. What if a few students learn something much faster than I thought they would?

The two principles that best address these questions are keys to success in a differentiated classroom in general: balance and flexibility. It's important to balance the needs of individuals and the group, and doing so requires flexibility.

In terms of individual assignments, it will always be the case that some students complete work before others do. It is therefore important to help students in a differentiated classroom understand at least two things about time and learning. First, make sure they understand that you expect them to do their best work on assignments, and that speed is not a goal. Be clear with students on what high-quality work looks like. When they submit assignments that are below that standard, give them back for revision and engage the student in a conversation about what else might be done to represent his or her best work.

Second, be sure students understand your belief that there are so many interesting and important things to learn that it's never correct to say they've finished learning. The first of the two principles can help students who hurry through tasks become more thoughtful about their work. The second helps develop a culture of curiosity and deep learning in the classroom rather than a sense that learning is about checking off assignments.

You should also be aware that if particular students consistently complete work earlier than everyone else, it's likely an indicator of one of two issues. First, the students may be doing their work too hastily rather than aiming for their best work. Second, tasks may be under-challenging for the student. A key goal of differentiation is to regularly provide each student with work that is a bit too hard for that student and with a support system to help them

> **It's important to balance the needs of individuals and the group, and doing so requires flexibility.**

"Good differentiation helps advanced learners encounter, succeed with, and ultimately embrace genuine challenge."

over the difficulty. It can be a challenge to address this goal with advanced learners, and as a result, those students can often complete work at a high level of quality with minimal effort. This pattern leads many very able students to fear and resist challenge because they've never learned to strive, struggle, and tolerate the kind of ambiguity that is inherent in challenge. Good differentiation helps advanced learners encounter, succeed with, and ultimately embrace genuine challenge.

Nonetheless, in a differentiated classroom, it is inevitable that students will complete assignments at varied times. An excellent response to this reality is to have anchor activities in place. An anchor activity, you will recall, is a learning option to which students automatically move when they complete an assigned task. See Chapter 3, pages 49–51, and Chapter 5, pages 86–89, for a detailed description and some examples of these activities.

To address the fact that some students may need additional time on a topic or skill when you feels it's necessary to move to the next component or unit, it's also important for you to become comfortable with teaching "backwards and forwards" simultaneously. Some strategies for helping some students fill learning gaps while continuing to challenge others are

- **Small-Group Instruction.** Students who need extra help work individually or in small groups with you to master essentials from the past, while other students work on new concepts or anchor activities.

- **Learning Contracts.** Instructional strategies such as learning contracts allow you to assign both common elements and individual-specific elements to students within the context of a shared format. For students with learning gaps, you can include on the contract some items that require practice with past essentials as well as some that require work with newly introduced content.

- **Centers.** Learning centers and interest centers can provide opportunities for students to work with both past and current content. Included in this category can be computers and other technologies that make available an increasing array of high-quality programs tailored to individual learning needs, particularly in the areas of literacy and numeracy. Students are typically assigned to various areas of the room in which particular tasks are located and asked to move among the areas and tasks over the course of one or more class periods.

- **Differentiated Homework.** When students struggle with work in school, those students' homework struggles are often amplified when the assignment is the same for everyone in a class. It can be far more useful to a student to do homework tailored for his or her particular learning needs at least some of the time. Providing time at home for students to practice with critical skills not mastered in the past is one way to tailor homework assignments.

- **Double Dipping.** Particularly in the elementary grades, teachers sometimes have multiple groups meeting around the same topic—for example, several reading groups or one group that meets with the teacher about math in the morning and another subject in the afternoon. It can be helpful to have students who need additional, well-focused work in a given area participate in two reading groups.

Managing the time of advanced learners can also be a significant issue in a differentiated classroom. You must be ready to help these students move ahead when they have mastered content, and also to focus on a particular area of interest when that seems appropriate. Here are a few points to consider in planning or managing time for advanced learners.

- Once a student demonstrates mastery of a topic, you no longer need to feel responsible for teaching that content to the student. As teachers, we sometimes feel like we're not doing our job unless we directly teach specified content to every learner. Let common sense prevail. We only need to teach what students don't know!

- Giving advanced learners more work than other students is not productive. It is burdensome rather than challenging. Instead, look for ways to challenge these students. Provide work that is more complex, open-ended, multi-faceted, or abstract. Such work may call on students to transfer ideas and skills to unfamiliar contexts, to use advanced resources to address real-world issues, or to use multiple skills to address a single problem. For example, if students are learning about simple machines, advanced students might be asked to look for applications of those machines in everyday tools and equipment.

If students are doing book reports, advanced students could be asked to show their understanding of the book by rewriting a scene in the book from the point of view of another character.

- Work that is appropriately challenging for advanced learners often stems from essential understandings (big ideas) or essential questions that are core to a topic or unit. Because big ideas or principles or essential understandings of a discipline are core to the meaning of that subject, there is always a more advanced version of them. Helping advanced students explore big ideas at a more sophisticated level enables you to keep the student connected to essential ideas shared by everyone in the class, but at an appropriate level of challenge.

- As a general rule, when a student demonstrates mastery in one content area, it's not imperative to extend the student's work in that content area. For example, if a student shows early mastery of content in a science unit but really wants to learn more about a topic in history, it's fine to develop work for the student in history (or invite the student to propose a topic or investigation). Many of the skills advanced learners use in substantial investigations—for example: research, writing, logical and/or creative thinking, reading, creating graphics to convey ideas—are useful across subjects. This is a chance to show students the connectedness of knowledge.

- It can be helpful to teachers and advanced learners to plan longer-term tasks or investigations rather than many shorter-term assignments. More complex assignments require more thought from advanced learners than is likely to be the case from a series of short tasks. Longer and more complex assignments also keep the teacher from having to find or create a new task each day for students who learn rapidly and/or in depth.

How Do I Control Noise and Movement?

Once again, balance and flexibility are important. A classroom full of young learners will never be (and should never be) sound-proof and wiggle-resistant. The goal in a differentiated classroom is not to prevent conversation and student movement in the classroom, but rather to shape it for the task at hand.

There are times when students should work silently. At other times, it's important for students to use very quiet voices to communicate with peers. At still other times, normal conversational voices are appropriate. At no time is shouting acceptable. Certainly you need to work with students to help them understand both when and why particular levels are effective. For example, you may explain that when you are working with a group of students, it's important for you to be able to hear them easily and for them to be able to hear you. Therefore, at those times, students doing other work will need to use "tiny voices." (Teachers of older students might call them "movie voices"—the volume you'd use in the movie theater to say something to a friend without bothering people around you.)

When students are told to work silently, you need to give reminders that silent doesn't mean whispering. It means no sound at all. It may also be necessary from time to time for you to give a quick reminder to reduce voice levels. The signal may be verbal, a quick flick of the light switch, a sound (such as two quick claps followed by three quick student claps), or any other agreed upon reminder to turn down the volume just a bit.

Similarly, in terms of student movement, there will be times when no one should be out of his or her seat. At other times, it will be appropriate for designated students to get or return materials or supplies for a group or to go to you to ask a question for the group. In other contexts, it will be acceptable for students to move purposefully to secure materials, turn in papers, get help from peers and so on.

Here are some strategies for helping students manage voice levels and movement in the classroom.

- Make sure assigned work is appropriate for the readiness levels of the students to whom it's assigned so that there will be less need for students to seek help.

- Make sure assigned work is interesting to and engaging for the students who are asked to do it.

- Be sure students understand expectations for movement and conversation in the particular context in which they are working and why the expected behaviors are important in supporting the success of each learner in the class.

- Practice routines that may be new or difficult for students to recall so they understand what to do in terms of movement and conversation in each routine.

- When students get it right, be sure to compliment them. When they don't, take time to talk with them about why it was difficult to meet the expectations and what both you and students can do to ensure success the next time.
- Make sure guidelines, rules, and routines are as simple and straightforward as possible, and that they exist to support student success.

Remember that there are some students who simply cannot sit for extended periods. In some cases, these students may have a diagnosis of attention deficit hyperactivity disorder. Other students with a similar need for movement may not have a diagnosis. Find ways to support these students. You may send them on errands, ask them to assist in the classroom, give students permission to stand as they work, or even have two seats assigned to the student so that he or she can move from one to the other. It's nearly always the case that other students understand the need for a given classmate to be up and about. Just be sure the student understands the responsibility to respect the needs of the teacher and peers as they are respectful of his/her needs.

> Make sure guidelines, rules and routines are as simple and straightforward as possible, and that they exist to support student success.

How Do I Get Started?

In some ways, of course, this book has already provided many of the answers to that question. To summarize, it's important to understand what differentiation is and why it can be helpful students. Its key principles should guide your decision-making and actions. It's important to prepare yourself to be a leader in a student-focused classroom. It's also important to prepare the students to be participants in making the classroom work, and to prepare the classroom environment to support increasing student independence and success. It's important to study students consistently to understand them as individuals in order to teach them more effectively. And finally, it's clearly critical to think through classroom routines and to prepare to teach students to use them efficiently and effectively.

Beyond those foundational areas of preparation, however, there are a few other pointers that can be helpful in beginning to guide and manage a differentiated classroom.

1 **Find your own pace for implementing differentiation.** Some teachers are quite successful establishing a broadly differentiated classroom in a very short period of time. Others feel the need to progress in a more stepwise fashion. If you are in the latter group, consider starting in just one class or subject area. You might select the subject or class in which you sense the greatest need for differentiation, or you might prefer to start with the subject in which you're most comfortable.

You might want to begin differentiating and managing differentiation with tasks that don't require group work or conversation. You might find it easier to differentiate for just a brief time span and to do so in the last portion of a class or time block. This way, if things are going as you'd hoped you have a built-in transition. What matters most is that you progress in developing your skills in a manner that is comfortable for you.

2 **Plan for success.** Take time to envision how you'd like a class to proceed so that you have a mental image of what you and your students are aiming for. As you plan, ask yourself, "What could go wrong here?" Then proactively plan to avoid those potential pitfalls with clear directions, modeling, practice, and so on. Be sure students know and understand what they need to do in order to be successful with both the work you ask them to do and the routines that support it. Have an "escape hatch" ready so that if there's a significant problem, you are ready to make a quick and smooth transition to another task. (The need to use the escape hatch rarely arises when teachers plan thoroughly, but it's comforting to have one in place.)

3 **Be reflective.** Watch the students while they work so that you have a clear sense of what's going well and where work is still needed to smooth out potential rough spots in working processes. End each class with a few minutes of de-briefing with students, both about what they are learning and how they are working. Share your pride in their success in handling routines when that's

warranted. Let them know when they are not doing their best with routines. Continue to teach and polish routines just as you do with students' content skills. Throughout the year, re-visit with the students the goal of creating a classroom that supports each person's maximum growth. Provide ongoing opportunities for students to provide input into how the classroom can work better to help them succeed. Take time to reflect on your own growth as a teacher. The best teachers learn from both successes and glitches. The goal is growth, not perfection.

4 **Establish partnerships with colleagues.** Talk with teachers who teach in a flexible, responsive, student-centered, or differentiated way in their classrooms. Observe them when you can. Ask them to plan with you, observe in your classroom, or co-teach. Being an active learner on behalf of your students yields great benefits for you as it does for the young people you teach.

5 **Establish partnerships with parents.** When parents know we are deeply invested in the success of their children, they are our best allies. Over time, teachers develop a breadth of knowledge about the age group that parents don't have. Parents, on the other hand, have a depth of knowledge about their own children that teachers don't have. The combination of a parent's deep knowledge about an individual child combined with a teacher's broad knowledge of an age group is a powerful force in supporting learning. Let parents know that your goal is to help their child have the very best school year possible, that you are continually checking to see how their child is faring with critical learning goals, and that when you see a need to adjust teaching and learning options to ensure their child's vigorous growth, you will do that. Let the parents know you want to tap into their child's interests to make learning more dynamic, and that you want to help their student become more and more aware of ways to learn that are personally effective. Invite their input. Then be sure to listen. Share your observations about their child. From time to time, you should be able to help parents understand

how to be more effective in their role. From time to time, they should be able to help you see how you can fulfill your role more effectively as well.

Knowing What Matters

The questions and answers in this section are just a small portion of those you will encounter as you continue to move toward your goal of differentiating your classroom. Just remember that the variety of students entering today's classrooms represent the full spectrum of needs and possibilities in the world as a whole. There are few challenges more substantial, and few more important, than teaching in a way that dignifies humanity and elevates the possibilities in every one of them. It appears increasingly clear that impersonalized, one-size-fits-all instruction fails too many, if not virtually all, students.

Differentiation is not a recipe—it is an idea, a frame for thinking about teaching and learning. It suggests that a teacher can actively and meaningfully address students' varied learning needs while maintaining a focus on critical content by developing an environment that invites and supports learning; establishing and conveying clarity about critical learning goals; monitoring student status relative to those goals; and tailoring teaching and learning plans as necessary to attend to student readiness, interest, and learning profile. Central to the idea of differentiation is students' participation in the success of their own learning and in the smooth functioning of classroom processes and routines. All of these elements call on a teacher to become increasingly comfortable and skilled in guiding a classroom that is both flexible and orderly—one that employs the classroom elements such as time, materials, space, and grouping for the benefit of individuals as well as the group.

Chapter 5 provides examples and resources that illustrate many of the key ideas discussed in the book so far. It is, in effect, a toolkit. We hope that it will be useful as you translate ideas from the book into your own classroom practice.

Chapter 5
Ideas Into Action

"To provide choices, we must first acknowledge that what students do determines what they learn and that they can find many ways to learn the same things. Variety in 'doing' is the only way I know to ensure constancy in learning."

Phillip Schlechty
Inventing Better Schools

Chapter 5 contains examples of some of the processes and strategies discussed in the first four chapters of the book and offers a wealth of additional ideas as well. To provide a context for what you will find here, we begin with an example of one teacher moving through pre-assessment and planning activities for her kindergarten class. The chapter then offers a variety of additional pre-assessment and anchor activities you can use in your own classroom, as well as other strategies for monitoring student progress and scaffolding success.

Differentiation in Action: Ms. Sanders's Classroom

Karen Sanders thought about the upcoming math unit she would be using with her kindergarten students. She knew from her work in screening all of the kindergarten students in her school that she could expect students to be at different places with their understanding, skill and background knowledge. However, she wanted to pinpoint exactly where her students were in terms of her learning goals. So, where should she begin?

Establishing Classroom Goals

Karen reflected on a unit she had taught before and one she believed was an appropriate for the beginning of the school year. She organized her planning around what she wanted her students to **Know**, **Understand** and Be Able to **Do [KUD]**. She developed her KUD by using her state and district standards along with several math resources she had accumulated over the years. After some thought, she decided on the following learning goals.

Know:	Key vocabulary: count, sets, many, number, amount, numbers 1-10
Understand:	Numbers show an amount or quantity of something and can be represented in different ways.
Do:	• Identify and count the number of objects in a set. • Determine the amount of objects needed to compose and decompose a set. • Write numbers 1-10. • Make sets of objects, given specific criteria.

Karen next had to decide how she would determine students' prior knowledge related to her learning goals. She wanted to develop a pre-assessment that was relatively easy to administer but that would help to identify what students already knew and did not know with regard to her number sense unit. She also wanted a pre-assessment that would help her get to know the students themselves—their likes and dislikes and favorite things. See Figure 5.1 on page 78 for the pre-assessment used.

Karen decided to give the pre-assessment in small groups while students were completing another task at their learning stations. They were asked to either write the number of objects that they had on their paper or to draw the correct number of objects to match the number on their paper. When they finished their work, Karen asked each student to draw on the back of their paper something they like that they have more than one of, and show how many they have (for example: pets, good friends, tennis shoes).

This last task had a double purpose. First, it would help Karen learn something about her students' interests. But it would also handle the issue of "ragged time," since it was likely that her students would finish their work at different times.

Number Sense

Pre-Assessment for _____

Numbers	Objects	Mastery Level ($\checkmark$+, $\checkmark$, or $\checkmark$-)
	🖍️🖍️🖍️🖍️🖍️	
4		
2		
	🧢🧢🧢	
	📕📕📕📕📕📕	
10		
	👟👟👟👟 👟👟👟👟	
7		
9		

Figure 5.1

Analyzing and Applying Information

After reviewing the pre-assessment, Karen found that she had ten students who knew their numbers 1-5, five students who knew their numbers 1-10, and five students who could say their numbers but could not match objects to a specific number or know how many objects it would take to make that number. She made the decision that she would continue to emphasize math ideas during her morning calendar routine for the entire group by asking questions such as the following that would cause students to use their number sense skills.

> *How many boys do we have in class today? How many girls?*
> *How many days have we been in school this week?*
> *How many students are having a birthday today?*
> *How many lunches are on the back table?*
> *How many classmates chose pizza today as their lunch choice?*

Karen also decided that in addition to her calendar time each day, she would hold small group sessions for students to address the readiness differences she found from the pre-assessment. Her tiered instruction groups are outlined in Figure 5.2. Note that all tasks cover the same understandings, are equally respectful and engaging, but reflect the skill differences identified during pre-assessment.

Orange Group

students who knew their numbers 1-5

- Built on what they already knew to identify the numbers 6-10
- Used and drew objects to make sets for numbers 1-10

Purple Group

students who knew their numbers 1-10

- Composed and decomposed sets of numbers using a variety of objects
- Used teacher-made flash cards to have students match up the number word, numeral, set of objects to help students make that connection

Green Group

students who could not yet identify their numbers 1-5

- Counted out or drew objects to match a specific number
- Used flash cards to match the number to the correct group of objects
- Practiced writing the numbers 1-5 using models to guide their work

Figure 5.2

Other Pre-Assessment Ideas

You have just read an example of how Karen Sanders determined her students' readiness for a lesson while also learning something about them as individuals. There are, of course, several other methods you can use to pre-assess students' readiness, interests, and learning profiles. Examples of these follow. You should also feel free to substitute your own knowledge and interest-based inventories, as well as any other assessment options you believe will help you know your students better and monitor learning progress. No matter what methods are used, students will soon understand that you care to learn about who they are, what they know, what they're interested in, and how they prefer to work.

Student Inventory

A getting-to-know-you pre-assessment inventory can reveal helpful data for you to use in your planning. The number of questions could be adjusted to fit the reading and writing levels of the class and the time of year the assessment is given. Examples of questions include

1 **My family consists of**_____
_____.

2 **My favorite subject in school is**_____
because_____.

3 **My least favorite subject in school is**_____
because_____.

4 **One rule that I think our class should have is**_____
because_____.

5 **When we can choose how we show what we have learned, my favorite way is**_____.

6 **It is easier for me to do my work when I can**_____.

7 **One fear I have about school is**_____.

8 **I am most proud of**_____
because_____.

9 **I think that the best thing that a teacher can do to help me be successful is**
_____.

Line 'Em Up!

An enjoyable activity that works well at the middle school level is Line 'Em Up! This activity involves all students standing somewhere on a line that you have made using masking tape that matches their agreement or disagreement with various statements that you read aloud. Here is an explanation of the activity including sample statements you might adopt or adapt for use with students in a math class.

1. Draw a line on the floor using masking tape.

2. Tell students that as you read each statement, they should stand on the left side of the line if they strongly agree with the statement or on the right side if they strongly disagree with the statement. If students do not feel strongly one way or another they can stand near the middle of the line.

   - I am really quick at solving word problems.
   - I learn best when I work in a small group with other classmates.
   - I am good at explaining how I got my answer to a problem.
   - I find it easy to remember vocabulary words.
   - I like using manipulatives to see how math ideas work.
   - I think that math homework is easy to do.
   - I like hands-on projects that let us do math and apply what we have learned.
   - I am very confident in converting decimals to fractions.
   - I am good at estimating answers to math questions in my head.

3. Take a digital photo of each grouping so that you can later show the class how they looked as a group for each statement. Place the photos on a poster highlighting the statements that the grouping represents.

4. On a rotating basis have students study the posters and ask them to draw conclusions about the results they believe are important for the classroom. You might have them complete a sentence starter such as the one that follows.

Since we are all similar and different in really important ways, I think it would be helpful if this year in our classroom we

Cube About You

This activity is a small construction project that asks students to form a cube that reveals information that is unique to them by coloring or designing six small squares of white paper or cardstock that you later help them tape or glue together to form a Cube About You. Once the cubes are complete, ask students to group themselves with others who have the same designed/colored cubed as they do. They will quickly find that everyone's cube is different.

This task can launch a wonderful discussion about why you might need to assign different tasks to different students at different times. You can follow such a discussion by asking students to share any worries or wishes they have about your potential response to their cubes. Some students may desire feedback from you regarding how you will use the information they provided on their cubes to help them experience a great school year. Figure 5.3 provides a template for the cube as well as sample questions that can be used.

What Do You Already Know?

Students can indicate prior knowledge before beginning a new topic or unit of study using an activity as simple as the one shown in Figure 5.4. The form could be shown using an overhead or digital projector while students record their responses on a sheet or index card.

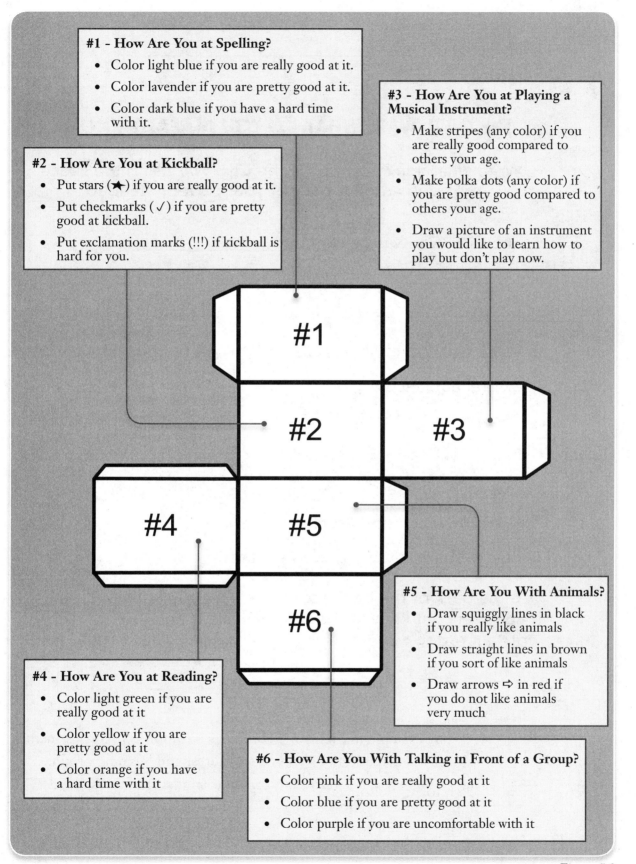

#1 - How Are You at Spelling?

- Color light blue if you are really good at it.
- Color lavender if you are pretty good at it.
- Color dark blue if you have a hard time with it.

#2 - How Are You at Kickball?

- Put stars (★) if you are really good at it.
- Put checkmarks (✓) if you are pretty good at kickball.
- Put exclamation marks (!!!) if kickball is hard for you.

#3 - How Are You at Playing a Musical Instrument?

- Make stripes (any color) if you are really good compared to others your age.
- Make polka dots (any color) if you are pretty good compared to others your age.
- Draw a picture of an instrument you would like to learn how to play but don't play now.

#4 - How Are You at Reading?

- Color light green if you are really good at it
- Color yellow if you are pretty good at it
- Color orange if you have a hard time with it

#5 - How Are You With Animals?

- Draw squiggly lines in black if you really like animals
- Draw straight lines in brown if you sort of like animals
- Draw arrows ⇨ in red if you do not like animals very much

#6 - How Are You With Talking in Front of a Group?

- Color pink if you are really good at it
- Color blue if you are pretty good at it
- Color purple if you are uncomfortable with it

Figure 5.3

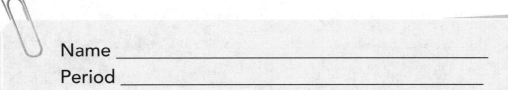

Name _____

Period _____

THE CIVIL WAR: WHAT DO YOU ALREADY KNOW?

Write what you know about the Civil War using the space provided and the back of your paper if needed.

1. The Civil War was caused by _____

_____

_____

2. Write what you know about the following people/events:

- Abraham Lincoln

- Harriet Tubman

- General Robert E. Lee

- General Ulysses S. Grant

- The Emancipation Proclamation

- Gettysburg (or any Civil War battle)

Use the back of the paper to share what you know. If you don't yet know about an item, list it and just write DKY (don't know yet).

Figure 5.4

The example in Figure 5.5 combines a readiness pre-assessment with additional questions related to interest and learning profile data. You may want to routinely include similar questions to aid in planning relevant learning experiences that are likely to engage students and promote learning.

Name _____

WHAT DO YOU KNOW ABOUT SIMPLE MACHINES?

For each simple machine, write all that you know in the space provided.		
Simple Machine	**What Does It Do?**	**Give an example using words and/or pictures**
1. Pulley		
2. Lever		
3. Wedge		
4. Wheel and Axle		
5. Inclined Plane		
6. Screw		

List 3 topics you would like to learn more about in our Simple Machines unit.

1. _____

2. _____

3. _____

Think about how you like to learn and place an X next to any statements that are true for you.

- I like working: __ by myself __ with a partner __ in a small group.

- I like to work: __ sitting at my desk __ at a table __ on the floor.

- __ I like to talk about what I know.

- __ I like to draw or illustrate what I know or ideas that I have.

- __ I can work when there is a little noise.

- __ I work best when it is quiet.

Another favorite way I like to learn is _____

_____.

Figure 5.5

Frayer Diagram

A Frayer diagram, shown in Figure 5.6, is a graphic organizer that can reveal what students already know or have learned about specific vocabulary, events, people, and concepts from any content area. It also allows students to write or draw what they know using abbreviated forms of language and/or illustrations, which can be particularly helpful with students who are learning English, those who have a preference for artistic expression, or those who have reading or writing difficulties.

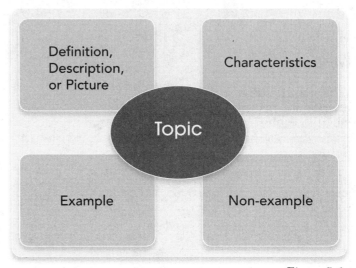

Figure 5.6

Anchor Activities

Another valuable tool in a differentiated classroom is anchor activities. An anchor activity is a purposeful learning experience that students can complete independently. It is instituted as a classroom routine, and can be used to

- extend or enrich students' interest in a topic;

- provide an opportunity for students to apply knowledge and skills;

- begin or end a class period;

- engage students after lunch or another transition; or

- direct students to a task to do when they finish an assignment and other classmates are still working.

The choices provided as anchor activities should be selected based on what students are currently able to do, and should be relevant to the topics studied in class and mindful of learners' interests and preferences. Effective teachers routinely change the options presented to students in order to keep students engaged and to reflect new skills and interests. Figure 5.7 provides of several examples of anchor options.

Anchor Option	Variation
Journal Prompts • Journal prompts are short writing assignments that cause students to reflect on what they have learned, make a connection to their lives, explain what they understand, note what is most important to know, or respond to a scenario in which they must generate possible solutions.	• Young students might reflect on what they think was the best part of a story, field trip, or experiment. • Older students might respond to scenarios or dilemmas that ask them to apply content knowledge and skill in a new context. For example, after a unit on the weather, a scenario asks them to generate a new warning system or evacuation plan.
Independent Reading • Teachers can provide a variety of reading materials that students are allowed to select for independent reading. • Some teachers might have a special location in the classroom where reading materials are stored—such as a basket, storage bin, or designated book shelves.	• Young children might have browsing boxes that contain books at their current reading level and also have an area of the room where books on a unit of study might be located. • Older students may chose to read a library book, a favorite magazine, or a newspaper. • How-to books might appeal to older students who want to increase their knowledge and skill on a particular topic—for example, how to build a rocket, how to plant a garden, how to fix a car.
Puzzles • A variety of puzzles is engaging for students of all ages. They can range from very simple, large wooden puzzles to complex crossword puzzles.	• Young students might have a designated activity table where puzzles are located nearby. • Sudoku, crosswords, or other puzzles can also be stored in large plastic bags or file folders; students could take puzzles to their desks to complete.

Figure 5.7

Anchor Option	Variation
Games • Board games, card games, flashcards, chess, concentration, and other games appeal to students of all ages. Many can be appropriate for skills practice and can be completed individually, in pairs, or small groups. • Wise teachers will give explicit directions regarding their expectation for noise and student conduct while they play games. It's a good idea to designate which games are allowed during particular time periods.	• Young students might use a number of matching games to practice skills, review vocabulary or math facts, and solidify what they have learned about a topic. • Older students do enjoy similar matching games for review of important facts, people, events, formulas, issues, and ideas. • You can easily make file-folder games for vocabulary or spelling review in which a student matches the word to a definition or its use.

Independent Projects
 	
• Independent student investigation on a topic of interest involves students in
 	
  ♦ conducting research using a variety of sources;
 	
  ♦ deciding how they would show what they have learned by making some kind of display or presentation; and
 	
  ♦ sharing the information with an appropriate audience.
 	
• Teachers are advised to establish timelines and benchmarks as indicators of quality work before the projects begin.
	• Younger students might be interested in researching information about an animal, famous person or place, or how something works.
	
	• Older students may be interested in investigating a topic related to a unit of study, a question that is related to their lives, or a topic they encountered while watching television, surfing the Internet, or reading a book or magazine.
	
	• Simple forms that help students manage their projects so that they remain focused and organized can be extremely useful to you and your students.
	
	• You may need to help students locate on-level resources that align to their topics of interest.
	
	• Check-in sessions are useful ways for students to receive feedback on the quality and progress of their work, as well as guidance on next steps.

Anchor Option	Variation
Test Prep Materials • Many schools purchase or have developed test preparation materials that help students review specific content and skills they have learned previously. • Students' preparation and confidence will improve if they can do their review using similar formats to those they will encounter on a formal assessment.	• For very young students, the test preparation materials may be simple tasks in which students fill in a score sheet and become familiar with how questions are asked on a standardized test. • Older students may use a packet of materials that matches the area in which they need more practice; then they may check their work against an answer key, record their progress, and note their next steps.
Computer Work • There are several computer programs that allow students to practice needed skills, read books or other documents, or learn important information about a topic by accessing sources on the Internet. • Students might be assigned a WebQuest to be completed over a specific time period that is connected to a unit of study or to a student's area of interest. • Students who have completed particular writing pieces and want to publish those could use computer time for that purpose.	• Students of all ages enjoy using the computer, but computer work can easily blend into computer play. Teachers are advised to set specific guidelines for approved, appropriate computer tasks. • If there are limited computers available for student use, you may specify how the computers will be shared so that everyone gets a turn. You can keep a timer to help control time management. • When students complete a task at a computer station as part of required class work, an anchor option could be to return to that task to gain additional practice (or just to allow students the opportunity to further enjoy using the technology).
Independent Writing • Students may keep a notebook to record thoughts, ideas, feelings, summaries, explanations, or other notes they wish to remember. • You may provide students with a list of writing choices in different genres, such as letters, poems, greeting cards, stories, reports, newspaper articles, blogs, scripts, graphic fiction, e-mails.	• Young students may need scaffolded writing prompts or product frames to consult for different writing tasks. • Older students may be allowed the anchor option of choosing their own favorite topic or genre to write in. • You could require that each student have one published piece of writing each marking period and students know that they can return to that writing any time an anchor option is available.

Anchor Activity Log

In order to keep track of anchor activities that students work on for a period of time, you might have students record their anchor activity work on a form or log. Students should also be able to do a self-evaluation regarding the quality of their efforts, using a +, ✓, or – to indicate good, acceptable, or weak effort. An example of a log is shown in Figure 5.8.

Anchor Activity Log for the Week of _____				
Name: Jean P.			**Class Period:** 2	
Monday **Short story work**	Tuesday **Short story work**	Wednesday **free reading**	Thursday **Short story work**	Friday **Short story work**
+	+	✓	–	+

Teacher Comments:

You chose your anchor options wisely this week and concentrated on them well. I agree with your self-rating.

Figure 5.8

Scaffolding Student Success

One of the best ways to ensure student success in a differentiated classroom is to continually monitor progress and provide help where it is needed. Following are some ways to do both.

Monitoring Student Progress

Keeping track of students' progress can be accomplished using numerous tools and strategies.

Tracking Chart. One tool is a teacher-made chart that lists standards or skills along the top of the page and the names of students down the left margin, leaving plenty of room in the spaces for teacher notes. If you are comfortable making tables on the computer, you can create and update the chart electronically.

However, the chart will be more easily used in the classroom if you attach it to a clipboard or staple it inside a file folder so that it can be easily retrieved when reviewing a student's coursework, conferencing with a student, or observing students working. Figure 5.9 provides a sample of a recording system you might use to track students' math skill progress in a middle school classroom.

4th Period	Ratios and Proportional Relationships	The Number System	Expressions and Equations
	• Understand ratio concepts and use ratio reasoning to solve problems	• Apply and extend previous understandings of multiplication and division to divide fractions by fractions • Multiply and divide multi-digit numbers and find common factors and multiples	• Reason about and solve one-variable equations and inequalities • Represent and analyze quantitative relationships between dependent and independent variables
Latonya B.	9-17 good reasoning evident when asked orally	(1) 10-3 skills test scored 94/100	(1) 11-4 could solve simple equations; ready for increase in challenge
Matt D.	9-20 written explanation is solid	(1) 10-3 skills test scored 64-100 (2) 10-10 skills test scored 76/100	
Aaron H.	9-17 reasoning is not yet evident	(1) 10-3 skills test scored 74/100	

Figure 5.9

RAFT Strips. If you're not fond of charts, a very different way to monitor student progress is by using RAFT strips. You may be familiar with RAFT as a way of structuring writing projects. The acronym refers to the **R**ole of the writer, the **A**udience, the **F**ormat, and the **T**opic. But a coordinated set of RAFT assignments, like the one shown in Figure 5.10, can be very effectively used as a pre-assessment, formative assessment, or summative assessment.

The key is to set up the strips so that no matter which one a student selects, he or she has to include the same knowledge, understanding, and skills that other students must include in their strips. This can be handled through directions that say to students that they can select the option that seems most interesting to them, but that their answers must include specific key vocabulary and big ideas or principles. If specific skills are a target, those should be reflected in the way the strips are crafted.

When that stability exists across all options, RAFT strips are a great way to differentiate assessments in that they allow students to focus on an interest and/or mode of expression that works for them while still ensuring that all students demonstrate their level of competence with the essential knowledge, understanding and skill.

ROLE	AUDIENCE	FORMAT	TOPIC
Plankton	Big Fish	A painting or drawing with an explanation	You'd all be in trouble without me!
Gardener	Things in the backyard	Conversation	Do you know how we all help each other?
Lion	Things in the Jungle	Thank you note	I was just thinking about how important you are to me.
Kid & Adult at the grocery store	Other kids	Sketches for a children's book	It's amazing how things in here are connected.
Directions: Please choose one of the four RAFT strips to show what you know about how a food chain works. Be sure to use as many of these words as possible in your work: producer, consumer, decomposer, herbivore, carnivore, omnivore, predator, prey.			

Figure 5.10

The Mini-Lesson: Responding to Students' Needs

Effective teachers routinely build into their day or week opportunities to observe students at work and are prepared to take note of students who may need additional explanation, practice, or support. They should be prepared to quickly call a group of students together for a short time and assist that group with a short segment of instruction—a mini-lesson.

For example, you might notice while walking around the room that several students are having difficulty completing a graphic organizer. Invite those students and any others who are uncertain about the accuracy of their work to meet you at a back table or come to a carpet area. You can then provide the needed assistance, answer questions, and assure students that they are on track.

Following is an example of a teacher's conversation with a small group of first-grade students who are comparing ants and butterflies by completing a Venn diagram. The idea is to have students understand that while all insects have common characteristics, specific insects can have unique features that distinguish them from one another.

Teacher:	Boys and girls, as I'm watching you work, I see that some of you are having a bit of trouble with the Venn diagram because you may not remember some information you need to complete it. I want to ask anyone who needs a quick refresher to complete their work to join me for a minute on the floor at the front of the room.
Teacher:	Who can tell me what you remember about our study of ants?
Jamie:	They have 6 legs.
Teacher:	You're correct Jamie! Good job remembering.
Roberto:	They have two antennae.
Teacher:	Wow, Roberto! You, too. I can see you were also paying attention.
Ivory:	But they don't have wings.

Phillip: Well, I think maybe some do.

Teacher: Great! I can tell that you're really trying to think carefully about what you know and all of you are on track to complete this assignment. Let me remind you about what this graphic organizer helps you do. On the left-hand side you put down all the facts that are true for ants and on the right-hand side put down all the facts that are true for butterflies.

Teacher: Does anyone remember what goes in the middle of our organizer? Can anyone think of at least one fact that is true for both? It is fine for you to look at the pictures I have here to help you.

Jada: They both have antennae!

Teacher: Good work Jada. Give me a thumbs up if you think you understand how to finish this work!

Getting Help

In addition to keeping an eye out for struggling students, you should provide all students with routines that enable them to seek help or find it on their own when they are "stuck."

Signal Colors. One method that a student can use to alert you when he or she needs help is a system of color-coded disks or cups that you can use to quickly see how students feel about their current work. Figure 5.11 shows an example of a poster that a teacher put up to remind students how to use their discs.

First-Aid Station. Another way to assist students while they are working is to set up a First-Aid Station where students can access tips for completing assignments or find annotated workbook pages that provide support. Figure 5.12 provides examples of the kinds of materials a student might find at a First-Aid Station for upper-elementary students.

FIRST AID

Ideas for Writing
- Tips for creating characters
- Ideas for settings
- Plot possibilities
- Dialogue suggestions

Steps for Conducting an Experiment
- Equipment lists
- Setup procedures
- Safety rules
- Tips on completing recording sheets

Math Tips
- Fact sheets
- Examples, rules, or algorithms
- Worksheets with reminders inserted

Computer Tips
- How to make a podcast
- How to organize a PowerPoint presentation
- How to edit video clips
- How to insert graphics in a Word document
- How to do simple calculations in Excel

Figure 5.12

A Closing Thought

A colleague recently wrote in an e-mail that he believes meaningful teaching not only reflects the skills we acquire, but also the person we seek to be. We hope the book has helped you extend your thinking about managing the details of the classroom. We hope, too, that it has encouraged you to reflect on the person you seek to be as you lead the young people you are privileged to teach, and whose lives you will inevitably shape. Refining the skills of teaching is a career-long process. Enjoy the challenge!

References

Dweck, C. (2006). *Mindset: The New Psychology of Success*. New York: Ballantine.

Dweck, C. (2000). *Self-theories: Their Role in Motivation, Personality, & Development*. Philadelphia: Taylor & Francis.

Schlechty, P. (1997). *Inventing Better Schools: An Action Plan for Educational Reform*. San Francisco: Jossey-Bass.

Sternberg, R. (1984). *Beyond IQ: A Triarchic Theory of Intelligence*. New York: Cambridge University Press.

Sternberg, R. (1987). *Successful Intelligence: How Practical and Creative Intelligence Determine Success in Life*. New York: Penguin Putnam.

Taba, H. (1971). *Curriculum Development: Theory and Practice*. New York: Harcourt.

Taba, H. (1962). *Curriculum and Practice*. New York: Harcourt, Brace, & World.

Additional Resources

Cummings, C. (1997). *Managing a Diverse Classroom*. Edmonds, WA: Teaching Inc.

Cummings, C. (2000). *Winning Strategies for Classroom Management*. Alexandria, VA: Association for Supervision and Curriculum Development.

Dweck, C. (2006). *Mindset: The New Psychology of Success*. New York: Random House.

Rothstein-Fisch, C., & Trumbull, E. (2008). *Managing Diverse Classrooms: How to Build on Students' Cultural Strengths*. Alexandria, VA: Association for Supervision and Curriculum Development.

Sousa, D., & Tomlinson, C. (2010). *Differentiation and the Brain: How Neuroscience Supports the Learner-Friendly Classroom*. Indianapolis, IN: Solution Tree.

Tomlinson, C. (1999). *The Differentiated Classroom: Responding to the Needs of all Learners*. Alexandria, VA: Association for Supervision and Curriculum Development.

Tomlinson, C. (2001). *How to Differentiate Instruction in Mixed-Ability Classrooms, (2nd Edition)*. Alexandria, VA: Association for Supervision and Curriculum Development.

Tomlinson, C. (2003). *Fulfilling the Promise of the Differentiated Classroom: Strategies and Tools for Responsive Teaching*. Alexandria, VA: Association for Supervision and Curriculum Development.

Tomlinson, C. & Eidson, C. (2003). *Differentiation in Practice, K–5: A Resource Guide for Differentiating Curriculum*. Alexandria, VA: Association for Supervision and Curriculum Development.

Tomlinson, C. & Eidson, C. (2003). *Differentiation in Practice, 5–9: A Resource Guide for Differentiating Curriculum*. Alexandria, VA: Association for Supervision and Curriculum Development.

Tomlinson, C., & Imbeau, M. (2010). *Leading and Managing a Differentiated Classroom*. Alexandria, VA: Association for Supervision and Curriculum Development.

Tomlinson, C., & McTighe, J. (2006). *Integrating Differentiated Instruction and Understanding by Design*. Alexandria, VA: Association for Supervision and Curriculum Development.

Differentiation Central. *www.differentiationcentral.com*